you can help
PUBLISHING

Mental Health *for* Men

Common problems ~ *practical solutions*

by John Ashfield PhD

Dr John Ashfield PhD
© YouCanHelp Publishing 2017
For further copies of this booklet
Contact: Phone 0439 692 975 **Email:** mcrafter@youcanhelp.com.au
Graphic design: Green Pigeon Graphics – Johanna Evans
General editing: Sharon Maree Crafter

Mental Health *for* Men

Common problems ~ *practical solutions*

by John Ashfield PhD

IMPORTANT NOTE

The information and ideas in this book are not intended as a substitute for medical or other forms of professional assessment, diagnosis, treatment, or therapy. Some of the information contained here will, over time, be subject to change due to advances in knowledge and changes in population health. In cases of physical or mental health difficulties, information and advice from a qualified medical practitioner should always be sought.

All responsibility for editorial matters rests with the author(s). Any views or opinions expressed or advice given are therefore not necessarily those of YouCanHelp Publishing. The information and/or self-help resources in this publication are not intended as a substitute for mental health assessment, medical or psychiatric consultation, assessment or treatment.

Contents

Contents

Introduction

This book deals with a range of topics important to male mental health, as well as some basic self-help strategies. But in case that sounds a bit tame, keep reading because it also dares to challenge several popular myths and stereotypes about male mental health, and tackles some hotly debated issues such as how we understand mental health, and the tendency of some mental health commentators, mental health professionals, and the mass media to unnecessarily medicalise mental health difficulties. The book also touches on the issue of services for men: how difficult it can be sometimes for men to obtain appropriate and confidential professional support when they need it.

Mental health difficulties mentioned in the book are those that are termed *high prevalence* difficulties – those that are most common and that affect a significant percentage of the male population. Less common and usually more serious mental health difficulties are not discussed here, both because they represent a quite small percentage of mental health difficulties overall, and because they have a degree of complexity that is best read about in more detail than space here allows.

Though this is clearly a book written for men, it will doubtless be of interest to women too: women who care about men, and whose own health and wellbeing is of course inseparable from that of the men in their lives.

True, False, and Somewhere In-between

There are more mental health difficulties amongst men than women
The prevalence of mental health difficulties amongst men is approximately equal to that of women

Men suffer from more depression than women
Twice as many women experience depression compared with men

After disaster situations (like bushfires and floods) men suffer more from PTSD than women
In general, at least twice as many women experience PTSD compared with men

Men attempt suicide at a higher rate than women
Women attempt suicide at a higher rate than men, but most men succeed on their first attempt

Men don't seek help when they experience mental health difficulties
When services that know how to engage with men are available and accessible to men, men do use them; men do seek help

If more men sought help with depression less of them would go on to end their lives
In many cases men who kill themselves do not have a depression or any history of depression or any other serious mental health difficulty. Many men who do kill themselves are experiencing situational distress, the significance of which may be overlooked if the emphasis of prevention is on depression or serious mental health difficulties

If men would seek help with mental health difficulties, they could easily receive professional support
Most men are prepared to seek help where appropriate services are accessible and available, but in places – especially rural and regional areas, male friendly services often don't exist, and standard mental health services (if they exist) may have long waiting lists and/or exclusionary eligibility criteria

Antidepressants reduce the incidence of suicide
Current evidence does not suggest that anti-depressants have an effect in reducing the risk of suicide attempts or completions

Current mental health campaigns that focus on reducing the stigma of mental health difficulties make things better for sufferers
There is still no convincing evidence to support this assertion. In fact, in some cases, because of their use of negative illness labels and language, such campaigns may prove to have made things more difficult for sufferers.

There is much debate about what *mental health* is. Is it a state of happiness, being able to cope and having a certain degree of self-confidence, or perhaps some state or degree of wellness or wellbeing? Some suggest it is simply the *absence* of mental illness.

The idea of *mental illness* is also hotly debated; though many mental health professionals, the media, and governments are prone to using the term as a 'catch all' phrase for any significantly challenging or troubling mixed experience of mind, thoughts, emotions, bodily sensations, or behaviours, other experts in the field strongly disagree. They argue that even the term *mental health* derives from and is the inevitable opposite of mental illness, and that the former would not exist without the latter.

Critics of the mental illness/mental health way of thinking argue that this wrongly frames ordinary, albeit sometimes very challenging and painful human experience or distress (which, yes, people will sometimes need help to get through) as illness, when it isn't illness at all. They argue that there is no such thing as mental illness only physical illness. If an organic, bio-chemical, or physical cause is responsible for disrupted emotional or mental functioning or behaving in a strange, dangerous, or self-defeating way, that is simply a physical illness or process that is having unwanted effects in a person's experience and behaviour, not a mental illness. Further, they argue that the very term mental illness tends to demean, depersonalise and label people, and creates conditions where they are perceived and responded to by society negatively, and viewed by mental health professionals more as objects than persons; objects of illness, diagnosis and treatment.

As you can see these aren't simple issues, and they affect men and women. However, it is important to take some kind of position on them if you are writing about men's mental health and trying to say something useful and helpful as this book endeavours to do. As you read on you will see the book shows sympathy for the critics of the orthodox view, whilst for practical purposes still using the term *mental health* and adopting the term *mental health difficulty*, so what is being discussed isn't too foreign or far removed from the current language being used by medical and mental health professionals; language that is now deeply embedded in the community psyche.

Put another way, the purpose of this compromise is to bridge the divide somewhat for ordinary readers, rather than using unrecognisable language and ways of talking about the broad spectrum of emotional and mental functioning psychiatrists refer to as *mental health problems, illness, or disorder*. But do take note of how this is done, because the motive here is to preserve men's dignity and enhance their wellbeing, whilst at the same time not trivialising the complex difficulties of some men, or of those whose experience on occasions is so painful, distressing, and seemingly inescapable, it can lead to potentially tragic consequences.

Defining what is Meant by *Mental Health Difficulty*

Anyone can experience a *mental health difficulty*; and everyone likely will at some stage of their lives. A mental health difficulty in most cases does not emanate from a physical illness or disorder. It is a common human *challenge* to be tackled creatively and constructively, including sometimes with the use of psychotherapy, and yes, medication, should that genuinely have something to contribute.

A *Low Intensity Mental Health Difficulty* interferes with a person's usual or preferred mental, emotional, and social capacity, and perhaps as well, their experience of feeling capable and competent.

Low intensity mental health difficulties are usually associated with major life changes and challenges, like: unemployment, sickness, loss and grief,

Low intensity mental health difficulties are usually associated with major life changes and challenges, like: unemployment, sickness, loss and grief, money troubles, relationship difficulties, conflict, and stress.

money troubles, relationship difficulties, conflict, and stress. Low intensity mental health difficulties are common and are usually resolved through a person's own coping ability, adjustments to lifestyle, and the support of friends and family. Of course, professional help may also be important, particularly if a person becomes 'stuck' and can't seem to recover or move forward.

> We need to dispense with demeaning labels and see mental health difficulties as a common part of our shared human existence.

A *High Intensity Mental Health Difficulty* usually significantly impairs a person's ability to function on a day to day basis and noticeably interferes with their usual or preferred mental, emotional, or social capacity, and their experience of feeling capable and competent.

Such a difficulty usually requires more than a person's own coping ability, lifestyle adjustments, and the support of friends and family. At least initially, it will usually require mapping and analysing by a qualified health professional (a doctor, psychotherapist, psychologist, or, in some cases a psychiatrist), who will also suggest and perhaps provide appropriate psychotherapy (psychological therapy).

In some cases, a General Medical Practitioner or Psychiatrist will also recommend prescription medication, which should be carefully considered for its potential to harm, evidence supporting its effectiveness (efficacy), and its appropriateness for the difficulty. If prescribed, it should be regularly reviewed both for any side-effects, and for whether it is genuinely helpful or still necessary.

Some 'Home Truths' about the 'Problem' of Stigma

In recent times, we've been bombarded with all kinds of media messages and images about 'mental illness' and 'mental disorder'. For some people who themselves *experience* mental health difficulties, this language of illness and disorder hardly makes them feel normal; in fact, it reinforces the very stigma that some mental health campaigns (which themselves use this language) claim to be addressing. One also has to wonder whether in fact we are becoming desensitised by too much 'marketed awareness', and not enough understanding – at least of a kind that is helpful?

What we do know, is that people fear what they don't understand. And given that mental health difficulties are mostly happening within a person's own experience rather than being exhibited in their behaviour or other outward signs, it is understandable that we have some trouble appreciating their significance, defining for ourselves what they are, and feeling comfortable in what is rather cloudy territory. All of this can interfere with how we usually like to 'size a person up' or read their mood and experience – something we are doing all the time in our relationships with others. What we can't easily make sense of, we can find unnerving and disquieting. And of course, someone else's experience of a mental health difficulty, should they happen to be a friend, family member, or partner, may by association, seem to imply something about us we would prefer it not to.

There is good reason then, why any public mental health promotion campaign will consider the importance of endeavouring to demystify mental health difficulties, providing people with up-to-date clear and accessible information; information communicated in a way that does not reinforce stigma, and that helps people feel more not less comfortable talking about mental health difficulties. The fact is, none of us are immune to such difficulties, they are common, and, more often than not, associated with adverse life experiences – something none of us are exempt from or privileged to escape.

As a community, we do need to become more comfortable talking about mental health difficulties and genuinely supportive of people who experience them. But when it comes to you as an individual talking about and disclosing your own emotions and very personal struggles and experience, a mental health difficulty perhaps, what then?

Each of us is entitled to personal privacy, and no, there should be no pressure to disclose anything you don't want to. Sure, there needs to be a public conversation about mental health difficulties, but when it comes to your personal mental health, it is up to you to choose what you disclose, to what degree and to whom.

Of course, if you're struggling to cope emotionally or psychologically and are developing or appear to have developed a real problem with your mental health, then you're best seeking out appropriate professional assistance and support. And when you do, you have every right to want to preserve your personal privacy, and to expect to be treated in a way that is sensitive to your male experience and needs.

Health professionals and service providers have an obligation to provide proper confidentiality to all clients, and an approach that is respectful, informed, and appropriate to them. That this doesn't always occur (and this is more of an issue for male clients) is precisely why some men don't seek support and assistance when they need to, and is why some service providers have a poor track record of engaging with men. So, you need to be an informed and discerning consumer, and on occasions may need to 'stick up for yourself'.

> Health professionals and service providers have an obligation to provide proper confidentiality to all clients, and an approach that is respectful, informed, and appropriate to them.

Examining venues where men must go to receive mental health support or psychological therapy, quickly reveals that confidentiality isn't what it should be. It may be compromised by having to attend appointments at a conspicuous public facility, sitting on display in a public waiting area, and then having one's name called out. Not quite what you'd expect confidentiality to look like. Sure, the notes the practitioner might take are confidential, and what is said in the interview room may be, but the rest of the experience can leave a lot to be desired. The effects of factors of this kind need to be understood for what they are and not conveniently hidden behind a more general notion of stigma.

> The effects of factors of this kind need to be understood for what they are and not conveniently hidden behind a more general notion of stigma.

Discussing mental health difficulties with a GP is favoured by some men for good reason, because though sitting in a public waiting area is quite uncomfortable for most men, at least in a general medical centre men can do so without anyone knowing why they are there. The challenge comes if the GP thinks referral to a psychotherapist, psychologist, or mental health practitioner is needful but such a service isn't offered discretely on the same premises. Incidentally, if you do go to see your GP about a mental health concern, be sure to book an extended or long appointment, so that your GP can give the time that is needed to properly hear and assess your needs.

If you are referred on by a GP for psychological or mental health support or therapy, don't hesitate to ask the GP about the approach the professional or agency to which you are being referred is known for in dealing with men. You might also like to ask the service provider how best they can ensure proper confidentiality for you. Yes, they may have to adjust their approach for you, and they may find this challenging, but they have a responsibility to provide a service to you that is in line with their *charter of healthcare rights*, or their *value statement* about client or patient confidentiality (nearly all services have these). It is time all of us started challenging the way men are dealt with, and the discrepancy between rhetoric and what happens in some places where services are offered.

If you are referred on by a GP for psychological or mental health support or therapy, don't hesitate to ask the GP about the approach the professional or agency to which you are being referred is known for in dealing with men.

One further issue to consider when it comes to cultivating a more public discussion of mental health difficulties, is the way in which current mental health literature and institutions communicate about them. Too often these difficulties are couched in technical terms, and are inappropriately described using the language of illness.

The bulk of mental health difficulties can be explained simply, and should not be considered or referred to as illnesses or disorders. It only serves to reinforce stigma when these difficulties are unnecessarily *medicalised* and *pathologised* (referred to and depicted as a disease),

The bulk of mental health difficulties can be explained simply, and should not be considered or referred to as illnesses or disorders.

rather than seen as a commonplace challenge that a good percentage of us will face at some time across our life-span.

Viewed as common and prevalent, and simply explained, mental health difficulties are more likely to become part of open community communication, and to elicit appropriate support for people experiencing them. We need to dispense with demeaning labels and see mental health difficulties as a common part of our shared human existence. As someone once said, 'Labels are for jars not people'.

> We need to dispense with demeaning labels and see mental health difficulties as a common part of our shared human existence.

Insiders admit, that the mental health 'system' and its approach is long overdue for an overhaul but is also strongly resistant to change. Be that as it may, each of us can contribute to a potent impetus for change, by becoming a little better informed about mental health and mental health difficulties, and by challenging language, labels, literature, slogans, and the practices of some service providers that do not show due concern or respect for human individuals experiencing difficulties to which all of us are potentially vulnerable.

Work and Play: Achieving a Sustainable Ratio

Doubtless you've heard a health or wellness commentator extolling the virtues of a 'work/life balance'? The phrase is so often mentioned, it has become rather trite and mentally dismissible like many other popular catchphrases. A reason it is easy to ignore is because of what it implies (even if it's not meant to), some sort of 50/50 balance of work and non-work, the latter being occupied with recreation, exercise, perhaps meditation, and the pursuit of personal

> There is of course considerable merit for self-preservation and self-care in achieving a better ratio and relationship of work versus non-work activities.

interests. Of course, such an idea is a nonsense for the vast majority of people who work full time and could not possibly contemplate such a luxury. Having said that, there is of course considerable merit for self-preservation and self-care in achieving a better ratio and relationship of work versus non-work activities.

Our work and our occupational projects may well be very important and meaningful for us, they may be what provides us with mental stimulation, social interaction and inclusion, and a daily sense of purpose that is fundamental to our lives. This isn't only true for men, increasingly it is true for many women as well. And, whilst we don't discount the value of other important elements of life – like exercise, relaxation, relationships and family, and our mental and emotional development, we may not have the most sustainable ratio of these elements happening for us. Fatigue, a high level of stress, diminishing quality of relationships, a decline in creative output, and depression may all be signs that we have yet to genuinely address this issue.

Fatigue, a high level of stress, diminishing quality of relationships, a decline in creative output, and depression may all be signs that we have yet to genuinely address this issue.

If we become too absorbed in our work or projects, vitally important though they may be, we can end up functioning out on the periphery of ourselves – out of touch with the part of us that is most perceptive and capable of deep feeling, pleasure, and simple reflective satisfaction. We can become like tourists in life: taking snap shots of things without really fully exploring, comprehending or experiencing them. We can become disconnected from our capacity for reading important emotional cues and signals in our relationships. Desensitised to the needs and feelings of others, we can become alienated from the very ones all our hard work may be meant to ultimately benefit.

The critical test is to step back from our work and projects and see how long we can bear it; to see if we have the capacity to relax, relieve stress, and focus on other priorities – especially relationships, without undue agitation, and with genuine and patient interest.

The critical test is to step back from our work and projects and see how long we can bear it.

If we can't, it's a clear indication that we may need to rethink and readjust our priorities.

Though what constitutes a sustainable ratio will be different for each of us, working out what may need to be given more attention, and in what way, will invariably require thoughtful, reflective and genuinely honest assessment.

One suggestion is to draw a bar graph, using the different height of several bars to indicate important areas of your life, and the current relative attention they receive. This can help put things into perspective, and indicate what needs attention and how much. The bars don't necessarily have to achieve an equal height. Rather, they need to achieve a relative height that fits with what you honestly and realistically consider to be the kind of ratio that is healthy for you, and is sustainable over time. Use a diary or calendar to indicate dates for periodic review.

The thing to remember about the ratio of these elements is that it isn't a constant; it will change as things change in life – so it needs to be periodically reassessed. But it's well worth the effort and, far from detracting from your work and projects, can breathe new life into them.

The thing to remember about the ratio of these elements is that it isn't a constant; it will change as things change in life – so it needs to be periodically reassessed.

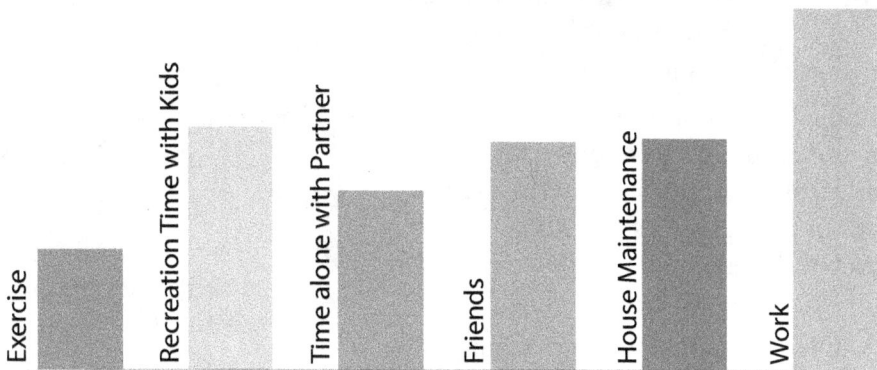

Important areas of your life, and the current relative attention they receive.

How to Avoid Being a Victim of Change

Adjusting to the pace of change in modern life can be very challenging. No small number of involuntary changes are foisted on us with the potential to produce all sorts of reactions in us. We may find ourselves feeling powerless, angry, anxious, and perhaps mentally overloaded and even somewhat 'paralysed'.

The world we once knew and which we counted on to remain largely the same, is changing fast, and we are faced with the considerable challenge of making the transition into a different future, and having to make lots of decisions that will determine its shape.

It goes without saying that we need first to have a clear and calm head to attempt this transition, and we may need to seek advice and support in a way we've never had to do before. This will invariably require us to be flexible, creative, and open – and maybe to a degree that is a bit challenging for us.

Without realising it sometimes, we can become rigidly attached to certain ideas, assumptions, routines, familiar patterns, and conventions – in the hope of maintaining life in a certain unchanged form. But is this good for us? As H.L. Mencken once said: "It is the dull man who is always sure, and the sure man who is always dull."

In the process of trying hard to maintain the status quo we can unwittingly imprison ourselves within our own insecurities, retarding our growth in resilience and our capacity for much needed new thinking.

> In the process of trying hard to maintain the status quo we can unwittingly imprison ourselves within our own insecurities, retarding our growth in resilience and our capacity for much needed new thinking.

And let's not overlook that coping with change and transitioning to something new, always involves some degree of loss (as the old gives way to the new) and consequent grief – grief that we must experience and deal with, not merely deny. Life simply can't progress or flourish otherwise.

Yes, this is all a very 'tall order' and it requires every bit of grit we can muster to get life on track – well a new track anyway. And we must make ready for the journey, by taking care of ourselves in ways perhaps that we have paid little attention to before, and by avoiding some things that are creeping into our lives that are unhelpful, like using too much alcohol, eating poorly, and not staying in good physical shape – all of which will likely have an impact on our mental health.

Making sure we get enough rest and exercise (most importantly that isn't associated with stressful work), that we manage stress through recreation and calming activities, and pay attention to our relationships, all are essential for coping and resilience.

Of course, change can turn out to be a real tonic. It can lift us out of a rut and present us with an opportunity to experience living more fully and humanly in the present moment, where we taste, see, hear, feel, and experience things with a whole new interest and intensity; things previously neglected or overlooked.

Perhaps the most important strategy for coping with change is to get back to our core values, and to focus on the people and things of most importance to us. We may need to become far less attached to the material things that are increasingly so subject to change – and that are so easily lost; instead, focusing more attention on cultivating whatever can nourish a stable sense of wellbeing, a sense of belonging, of caring and having others care about us.

Perhaps the most important strategy for coping with change is to get back to our core values, and to focus on the people and things of most importance to us.

Properly nurtured, these things can provide us with the dependable inner resources to help keep life hopeful, meaningful, and functioning in perspective. They can provide us with 'psychological buoyancy', a place to go when we need to 'catch our breath', and the emotional resilience to avoid being intimidated or overwhelmed by change now and in the future.

Providing Leadership in a Time of Crisis

Anticipating the likely effects of climate change, the potential of disease contagion, and especially the threat of terrorism, governments are busy formulating a whole raft of contingency plans to afford their citizens whatever protection they can. Whilst none of us (for the sake of our own mental health) can afford to become too preoccupied with thoughts of catastrophe or feelings of dread, reviewing our readiness to respond effectively to crisis and disaster certainly makes good sense.

Of course, few rural or regional communities are strangers to disastrous events, having contended with bushfires, droughts, floods, destructive winds, and country motor vehicle tragedies, just to name a few. Such communities are renowned for how they can usually pull together rapidly, in co-operative and practical ways. However, they're not always confident in their ability to deal with the psychological dimension of a disaster and its aftermath. And yet even this is largely within the capacity of communities, if those in leadership possess some basic knowledge of what is most helpful.

Experience of past disasters suggests that mental health services and counselling do have their place, but mostly well 'after the dust has settled' and, even then, mainly to help clarify and normalise people's experience – rather than dealing with mental health difficulties. In fact, the majority of people recover fully, with the support of their own families and communities, in six to sixteen months. Of those who do need assistance with a mental health difficulty (and 90% do not), most fully recover in twelve to twenty-four months.

Different kinds of disasters affect individuals and communities in different ways and to different degrees. But what

Different kinds of disasters affect individuals and communities in different ways and to different degrees. But what we do know is that people's ability to cope and adjust psychologically depends mostly on them getting the right kinds of immediate support.

we do know is that people's ability to cope and adjust psychologically depends mostly on them getting the right kinds of immediate support. Effective supportive actions include:

◆ Comforting, consoling, and listening to people who are distressed, and helping them to feel safe – including from further threat and distress

◆ Providing simple, brief, accurate and relevant information – especially about their loved ones

◆ Doing everything possible to quickly reunite people with their loved ones

◆ Helping people to become oriented to the reality of the situation, and play a part in their own return to functioning and feeling in control, by helping them to participate in simple but useful tasks

◆ Ensuring that people's practical and physical needs are met (food, sanitation, shelter, clothing)

◆ Ensuring that people have opportunities to share/talk about their experience – but this shouldn't be expected or forced

◆ Promptly linking people to systems of support and assistance, whilst ensuring that these are delivered in a way that is respectful and appropriate

◆ Offering to arrange professional support for people exhibiting unrelenting stress or anxiety, or who appear not to be recovering from the acute phase of the disaster

Providing leadership in a crisis by focusing on these essential measures can have a huge impact on people's natural recovery and healthy long-term adjustment.

Taking Care of Yourself After a Crisis

Australian bushfire disasters demonstrate over and over just how resourceful Australian men can be when 'their backs are to the wall'. Firefighters, landholders, and volunteers alike, even when their lives are at risk, press on unhesitatingly and relentlessly. They do what men have always done best: they suppress their fears, and distance themselves from the emotional content of their own experience, to be undistracted in their effort to impose control over the destructive forces and chaos threatening their communities and families.

Few examples better reveal how men 'not being in touch with their emotions', and being able to remain task focused and clear-headed in a crisis, are an indispensable asset to human survival. And, contrary to popular misconception, data on post-disaster mental health difficulties suggest that most men cope at least as well or generally better than women do, despite equal or greater exposure to dangerous, distressing and life threatening circumstances.

Few examples better reveal how men 'not being in touch with their emotions', and being able to remain task focused and clear-headed in a crisis, are an indispensable asset to human survival.

Some men do of course run into trouble. Strictly regulating emotions and thoughts that might impede one's capacity to respond to a crisis – putting them on hold, to be dealt with once threat and danger have passed, can result in some potential psychological challenges later on. Problems that may later emerge include:

- Suppressing or shutting out emotions long after doing so is needed or serves any positive purpose. It may be necessary to make a conscious effort to reconnect with and work through emotions put on hold, by taking time out to be reflective, and allowing thoughts and feelings to emerge and to be fully felt
- Struggling to relax, or to make time for proper rest; being locked into restless activity. Whilst men resolve emotions often by 'pushing them out' into physical activity, obsessive activity may be a way of avoiding dealing with feelings that are 'calling out for attention'
- Staying at home or withdrawing from usual social activities and social contact – especially with friends, is commonly a sign of not coping, and of emerging depression or anxiety. Confiding in a friend, talking about issues, and staying socially involved can be very healing and are vital to maintaining mental health. Activating our social brain – the cluster of brain activation areas that light up when we are sociable, can make mood buoyant and reduce anxiety and stress
- Increased alcohol intake. A more than moderate alcohol intake serves only to aggravate the symptoms of not coping, and diminishes the quality of much-needed sleep

- Too little sleep. Sleep, and plenty of it needs to be a high priority. It is restorative – boosting mood and energy and promoting physical and 'inner' healing. It is also the time when our experiences and memories are processed in the most helpful way. Sleeping in and early nights aren't being lazy or slack, they are crucial at times of ongoing stress

As men, we can weather most crises and difficulties very well. But there are limits to what we can cope with alone. We owe it to ourselves and to our families to seek assistance long before we experience being overwhelmed.

Why Wild and Natural Places are Good for Your Head

There is little doubt that men are attracted to the outdoors – to wild places, much more commonly than women are. And whilst some men venture there for the primal pursuits of hunting, fishing, and adventuring, their attraction to the wild is more complex than is generally realised. Getting out on the boat or 'going bush' might also be an important way for men to preserve or repair their mental health.

Few men are content with either the comfort of domesticity, or the constant 'drivenness' of modern life. For many, the experience of finding themselves in an over-constructed life is suffocating and stressful. There is always the longing, the "dream of breaking free and escaping to a 'man's place' under open sky, a place where physical strength counts and clocks do not dictate the rhythm of the day". Only here, in the wild places, can a man "sense the truth of being a man" say philosophers Sam Keen and Wendell Berry.

At a time when we appear most 'hell-bent' on wrecking natural environments, we probably need them more than ever before. They may be the only antidote to our increasing sense of alienation, and the effects of having to deal with too much information, too many stress inducing stimuli, and the fatigue both can cause.

There is in fact a strong body of research now suggesting that contact with nature leads to increased psychological health. Outdoor and wilderness recreation is well known for providing benefits of stress reduction, and for reinforcing a sense of connectedness, wholeness, and meaningfulness – all essential elements of mental and psychological health.

There is of course a deep bond and reciprocal relationship between humans and nature. This has been recognised in therapy with grieving men, who have reported experiencing the horizons of their previously 'closed in' and depressive 'world' (due to grief) expanding, in response to spacious environments of bushland, desert, or sea. In the solitude of natural environments men can often relinquish anxiety ridden attempts at control, can relax, be more fully themselves, and can trust themselves to the greater whole of which they sense they are a natural and accepted part. Nature is perhaps our most constant and reliable 'home and family'. Its amazing integration and coherence can bestow upon us a greater capacity of psychological integration and coherence.

As men, we need wild and natural places – not as a way of escape, but as environments in which we can mentally and emotionally heal and recuperate; places where, for a time, we can be more fully ourselves, reflective, feeling, and fierce; places where we can reunite with our best intentions, values and aspirations, and sense again the truth that being a man is good, and that we ourselves are worthwhile. It is the wild and natural places that can help us retrieve the humanness that is so important to us living our lives with genuine integrity.

> At a time when we appear most 'hell-bent' on wrecking natural environments, we probably need them more than ever before.

> As men, we need wild and natural places – not as a way of escape, but as environments in which we can mentally and emotionally heal and recuperate.

Being Sociable is a Tonic for Mental Health

Millennia ago the author of Ecclesiastes – believed to be King Solomon, said that, "a faithful friend is the medicine of life". Turns out he was spot on. Modern research has confirmed that social support has a powerful protective effect on health – it can potentially add years to your life.

Having people to confide in – people who are available to provide emotional support and with whom we can share social activities – boosts the body's immune system, acts as a buffer against the effects of stress on health, and is protective of mental health. Being isolated, and cut off from friends and social support, is associated with higher levels of depression, and higher levels of disability due to chronic disease.

> Being isolated, and cut off from friends and social support, is associated with higher levels of depression, and higher levels of disability due to chronic disease.

There is now evidence that men who lack social support, and are socially isolated, are at greater risk of developing coronary heart disease, and have from two to five times the risk of dying from all causes, compared to men who have strong social ties.

What is seldom recognised about social support is that, just as men and women are brought up and conditioned in significantly different male/female cultural domains, so too, what constitutes meaningful and helpful social support for each may also be different – and often is. For example, women tend to feel close to and supported by other women when there's an opportunity to be self-disclosing – through verbal and emotional expression. For women, shared activities are an opportunity for verbal intimacy. But for men, social support is experienced more through activities like working or playing side by side. Such activities in themselves constitute support. Even when men comfort each other in a crisis, it is physical presence that matters most to them, not intimate talk. Male communication is often different as well; though generally characterised by economy, it's no less meaningful or self-disclosing than female communication. It simply uses different devices, like yarns, humour, metaphors, and even insults.

Men can benefit greatly from the support that only other men can provide. Who else but other men know the experience of, or understand the issues of masculinity and manhood?

Unfortunately, one of the excesses of modern 'political correctness' has been to undermine and foster suspicion about male-only groups and activities. Yet it is these settings that have provided a safe male 'ritual space', permitting men, in their own unique ways, to display vulnerability, engage in self-disclosure, work through personal issues, develop emotional ties, and accept support from those who understand them most.

Of course, we should be attentive to the needs of our spouse or partner and our children – they need us as a mainstay and support, but we need make no apology for also wanting and seeking social support of the kind that can only be found in all-male company and activities.

Men can benefit greatly from the support that only other men can provide. Who else but other men know the experience of, or understand the issues of masculinity and manhood?

Talking Sense about Men and Feelings

For decades, men have been exhorted to "get in touch with their feelings", and to emulate women's ways of doing things emotionally, as the preferred model of what it means to be a 'whole person'. Some authors, on the subject of gender, lament that men can't express emotion in the easy and automatic way that women can. What seems not to have occurred to them is that men don't do this because they are not women!

For decades, men have been exhorted to "get in touch with their feelings", and to emulate women's ways of doing things emotionally, as the preferred model of what it means to be a 'whole person'.

In the dark past of gender relations, it was believed that women were 'naturally' inferior to men, and were put on earth for sex, reproduction, and domestic chores – an idea quite rightly overturned by the women's movement, to the benefit of us all. However, before there was time to draw breath, a new and aggressive brand of gender politics arrived, championing the 'truth' that the only significant difference between men and women is in sexual and reproductive function. How men and women think and feel and behave is all socially constructed, we were told.

Certainly, we are profoundly influenced by what we learn socially and culturally. But we now know, from a large body of scientific evidence, that differences in male/female roles, temperament and behaviour, have much more to do with our brain 'hardwiring' and hormones. The old notion of gender superiority needed to be dismissed. But difference is here to stay, and we better try to understand it.

One major difference that is evident, is in how men and women express and deal with emotions. Women tend (on average) to be better than men at expressing, remembering and verbalising emotion; they also tend to ruminate, or go over and over problems and their associated feelings – the pit-fall of which can be 'under-regulation' of thoughts and emotions.

Men, particularly in circumstances that prompt a protective response, prefer to spring into action and start problem solving. They appear to be better at emotion and thought regulation, paying less attention to them, and putting them on hold, to be dealt with when a perceived threat or danger has passed. The pit-fall for men can be 'over-regulation'; they can become disconnected from their emotions, or fail to deal with emotions put on hold. In these characteristic ways, both women *and* men can run into trouble.

Men, particularly in circumstances that prompt a protective response, prefer to spring into action and start problem solving.

These different emotional styles fit with the kind of action/task versus relationship-oriented roles towards which men and women tend to gravitate. And whilst culture certainly plays a part, biology and its strategies of survival appear to be both primary, and remarkably resistant to attempts at socially engineered change.

It goes without saying that men can learn to be better partners and lovers; able to listen, show tenderness, and communicate effectively. So long as we remember that men are not women, and that differences in verbal and emotional expression between men and women (no matter how infuriating sometimes) have served us well for a very long time, and for the foreseeable future will persist.

'Nip it in the Bud': Stepping in Early with Personal Problems

For most men, seeking help with personal problems doesn't come naturally. It can seem easier to postpone action until every bit of their capacity to cope is exhausted, or the earnest prompting of a partner can't be ignored any longer. Whilst there are understandable reasons why men often hold out in this way, there are some real benefits for men in stepping in early with personal problems, and seeking help well before feeling overwhelmed by them.

As men, we may have to override some powerful instincts to seek assistance because it isn't consistent with what we expect of ourselves, or with what is generally expected of us and our male role, to give leeway to personal vulnerability. Yet that is precisely why seeking assistance early is so important. If we take the initiative in getting help with personal problems before we are overwhelmed by them (and lose control over how public they become), we can deal with them in a way that is least likely to demean our maleness, compromise our privacy, or cause embarrassment. We can more thoughtfully seek the kind of assistance we need, and be in control of the process, instead of feeling as though others are having a field day with our personal issues.

If we wait to become emotionally destabilised and overwhelmed by a personal problem before seeking assistance, we may find ourselves either maneuvered (by well-meaning others) into, or having to accept, a form of assistance that cares little about preserving our masculine dignity.

Research has shown that men are less likely than their female counterparts to receive much needed assistance with personal problems, because many health and welfare services and professionals

> If we wait to become emotionally destabilized and overwhelmed by a personal problem before seeking assistance, we may find ourselves either maneuvered (by well-meaning others) into, or having to accept, a form of assistance that cares little about preserving our masculine dignity.

are not yet knowledgeable or skilled in engaging and working with men appropriately. Responding early to personal problems can buy time to 'ask around' – to find a counsellor or psychotherapist who doesn't have a gender-biased 'axe to grind', and who is competent and capable of working respectfully and effectively with men.

Another reluctance men commonly must overcome is investing the necessary time and money in the process of getting things properly back on track. Just as recovery from a physical ailment may demand time and expense, the same is often true of emotional and psychological ailments.

As men, we need to be as pragmatic about our psychological health as we are with other practical matters. Saying, "I need to get some advice about a personal issue" may well feel uncomfortable, but at least it leaves us in control, and free to decide how we will respond.

> As men, we need to be as pragmatic about our psychological health as we are with other practical matters.

'Biting the bullet' and seeking assistance early makes a whole lot more sense than waiting until a major crisis occurs – which may not only take much more time and effort to remedy, but can unnecessarily compromise both our privacy and our sense of manhood.

Is Counselling of Any Use to Men?

Well, a lot of men don't think so – and some of them for good reason. And let's not mince words here: some counsellors should not be counselling men. But there are good counsellors, and many men benefit enormously from counselling. In a survey of 650 Australian companies, men were a found to use workplace counselling more than women – especially for relationship problems and issues of stress.

There's no doubt that counselling can be useful for getting some perspective on things, and discovering our blind spots. It's also an excellent tool for making sense of our experience and thoughts which, if left to swirl around in our heads, can damage our mental health.

> There's no doubt that counselling can be useful for getting some perspective on things, and discovering our blind spots.

What should you look for in a counsellor? Any counsellor worth their salt should go to a lot of trouble to make you feel comfortable, psychologically 'safe', valued and respected. They will also understand the importance of building a good working relationship with you. In fact, relationship is a big part of the therapy of counselling; it's almost more important than anything else. A skilled counsellor will also ask you what *you* hope to achieve from counselling, and roughly how you think they may be able to help. And you have every right to expect that your experience, how you have come to view the world, and who you are as a person, will be considered vitally important in any process of trying to help you.

A good counsellor should also be reluctant to give advice, because men seeking counselling benefit most not from advice, but from information – relevant information that can be used for making sense of problems, making informed decisions, and getting on with problem solving and change.

Most men have little time for the sort of counselling that seems endlessly circular, keeps raking over feelings, and doesn't give something to work with. And that's fine. What you will probably find helpful though is to have a go at getting inside your experience – but in your words, in your way, and at your own pace. It really pays to get involved and steer things in the direction you want them to go, because how you experience the process of counselling, and how involved you get, are the two things that will most determine how well it works for you.

> Most men have little time for the sort of counselling that seems endlessly circular, keeps raking over feelings, and doesn't give something to work with.

It's perfectly reasonable, when considering whether or not to see a particular counsellor, to ask them whether they have a good grasp of men's issues and psychology. This goes for male or female counsellors.

If you are thinking about counselling, remember it has a lot to offer, but you will have to make it work for you. And there is nothing to stop you asking around, to find out who has a good track record.

Why Experiencing Powerlessness can be Poison for Men's Mental Health

For men, feeling powerless, and perceiving themselves to be powerless, is frequently associated with chronic stress, a decline in mental capacity (thinking, problem solving, memory recall), irritability, anger, and diminished verbal communication; which is why the effects of powerlessness in a man's experience and behaviour are sometimes confused with depression.

As males, experiencing powerlessness runs contrary to our hardwired action orientation and our inherent need to be a cause that brings about an effect. It is also contrary to the roles that are socially reinforced and demanded of us.

A number of circumstances and situational crises can give rise to feeling powerless. Some examples include: financial pressure or loss, unemployment or underemployment, relationship difficulties, seeing others distressed or upset in some way and not knowing how to respond, feeling dominated or controlled by another person, a change in health status, having a sick child or partner, chronic pain, loss or bereavement, being on the land and affected by drought, fire, flood, or pests, or perhaps a significant loss of status, role, or position, or having unmet expectations of a person or situation (whether realistic or not).

Lots of other examples could be given, but it's important to understand that you can feel powerless sometimes without knowing what's 'eating you'. You may need some help to track down and name what it is that's giving rise to your experience of powerlessness. This is important, because powerlessness may be an early warning sign that your mental health is in jeopardy; a signal that you might need to seek out some help to get on top of it.

A good starting point with this might be to ask yourself: "How might I be feeling powerless right now? In what ways?"

Depending on the circumstances, *structured problem solving*, combined with sound information and appropriate professional advice (which might be financial, legal, or of some other nature), can quickly restore a sense of being back in control.

As males, experiencing powerlessness runs contrary to our hardwired action orientation and our inherent need to be a cause that brings about an effect.

powerlessness may be an early warning sign that your mental health is in jeopardy; a signal that you might need to seek out some help to get on top of it.

The difference between *informal* 'on the run' problem solving versus *formal* structured problem solving is that *formal* problem solving involves a process with a set of steps and is usually written down. It involves gathering facts about the issue or problem at hand, brain storming options, thinking about the implications of acting on these options, selecting the best or preferred one and then acting on it. Just to go through this process, even in the absence of a desirable option, can be empowering – can give a sense of being less out of control. However, there is always something that can be done about a problem, even if that is to decide to frame and respond to it differently.

An impasse of powerlessness can often be broken simply by discovering a more helpful and meaningful way of thinking about a situation. Not only so, but to understand and to make better sense of things provides a much better basis for action. And taking some sort of action is the key here, because even a small act of power can have a disproportionately positive effect on your experience of powerlessness.

> And taking some sort of action is the key here, because even a small act of power can have a disproportionately positive effect on your experience of powerlessness.

Though circumstances may appear to have impoverished your options, there is generally always a choice you can make that can counterbalance your sense of powerlessness, impotence, and feeling inescapably overwhelmed. If you're too tired, anxious, or preoccupied to identify and deal with this yourself, and can't move beyond your present experience, you'll need someone else to help you with this, whether a trusted friend, or a psychotherapist, psychologist or counsellor that has a good understanding of male psychology.

A word of caution here: a severe or ongoing sense of powerlessness, is sometimes associated with men getting to a place of feeling suicidal and having thoughts of suicide. Powerlessness needs to be taken seriously – just as seriously as a condition of severe depression.

Stress: The Predator Within

Everyone knows what it's like to experience stress. And most people would agree that it usually isn't very pleasant. Not surprisingly, our stress now supports a growth industry, which markets stress reduction workshops, massage, supplements, and all manner of online relaxation resources. But few people fully understand the nature of stress, its effects, and the significant difference in the way it is experienced by men and women, and how this is exhibited in behavior.

The 'stress response' has its origins in our primitive past – when our ancestors frequently faced dangerous predators or enemies. It provided quick bursts of energy, strength and alertness, needed to stand and fight – or run away. Still 'wired' into our brains today, it involves a complex array of chemical reactions and changes in body function. Trouble is, because the mundane aggravations of daily life can also activate the stress response, we experience the same surge of body chemicals and changes in body function, designed for much less frequent major threats. Stressed too frequently, or for prolonged periods, our bodies take a terrible pounding.

This biochemical onslaught can compromise our immune system, making us vulnerable to infection and disease – including cancer. Hormones unleashed by stress can damage the digestive tract and lungs; they can also weaken the heart, leading to stroke and heart disease. Prolonged stress can eat away at every body system like an internal predator. Though it can protect us, it can also turn on us.

> Prolonged stress can eat away at every body system like an internal predator. Though it can protect us, it can also turn on us.

Recent research indicates that some people are more prone to stress than others. Losing a parent, being traumatised, or in some other way being exposed to a high level of stress in childhood, may permanently rewire the brain circuitry, making it much more difficult to deal with everyday stress in later life. But whatever our individual tolerance for stress, it can – and needs to be managed.

Unfortunately, amongst the first casualties of stress with men may be: communication, sensitivity, patience, empathy, and being sociable – and it's important to understand why.

Both men and women experience the stress response, or 'fight or flight' response, but then something surprisingly different happens. In women, a hormone call oxytocin is secreted which, in combination with and boosted by the female sex hormone estrogen, has not only a calming effect, but prompts them to be more empathic, nurturing and sociable. This has been termed the 'tend and befriend response'. In addition, women benefit from being emotionally and verbally expressive, and seeking empathy from others. Their ability to read others' emotional cues – such as facial cues, becomes enhanced.

In contrast, men not only experience the 'fight or flight' response, but they register higher levels of stress hormones (adrenaline and cortisol), which stay in their system longer. The male sex hormone testosterone inhibits oxytocin release under conditions of stress, which, along with stress hormones, promotes less social and more aggressive task-focused behaviours. Males become less sociable, have a diminished capacity for empathy, and have difficulty reading others' facial expressions – important for appreciating others' emotional experience. Under conditions of acute and chronic stress, males may tend to be more reactive, irritable, angry, argumentative, and less communicative and sensitive towards others.

The male response to stress may also help to explain why alcohol misuse, as a form of self-medication for the relief of stress, is a predominantly male behavior, one which is known to trigger or worsen mental health difficulties such as insomnia and depression. Men who drink alcohol

Unfortunately, amongst the first casualties of stress with men may be: communication, sensitivity, patience, empathy, and being sociable – and it's important to understand why.

In contrast, men not only experience the 'fight or flight' response, but they register higher levels of stress hormones (adrenaline and cortisol), which stay in their system longer.

immoderately (compared to abstinence) are also at much greater risk of suicide (some estimates suggest 90 times greater risk).

Again, in contrast to women, men characteristically benefit less from being verbally and emotionally expressive, and more from sharing tasks with other males and just being alongside them. For males, emotion and stress are often dispersed through action, physical activity, and practical tasks.

The male response to stress may also help to explain why alcohol misuse, as a form of self-medication for the relief of stress, is a predominantly male behavior,

It can help in understanding these male/female differences under stress, if we consider our hunter/gatherer past. Imagine a community under threat from a marauding tribe: the men would naturally be at the forefront in fighting off the aggressors, and to do so they would need to be fueled by hormones and energy boosting adrenalin until the job was done. It might put them and the community at greater risk and result in defeat, if they were to view their aggressors with empathy, or to pay attention to anything other than aggressively pursuing the task at hand: defeating their enemies.

Women in these circumstances would also have needed the whole of body system activating effects of the 'fight or flight' response – at least at first, but then an enhanced sense of the need to affiliate with other women to protect the welfare of offspring, and to provision their male protectors so that the whole community had the best chance of survival. It is interesting to note that in situations of disaster, community trauma, and adverse climatic events, these stress responses are still largely true to form and are our default settings.

It is interesting to note that in situations of disaster, community trauma, and adverse climatic events, these stress responses are still largely true to form and are our default settings.

Even when men and women experience moderate degrees of stress, the characteristic male and female responses will often become evident. Of course, stress is still an individual experience, which varies from one individual to another, and there will also be exceptions to the rule when it comes to on-average male and female responses to stress. Notwithstanding this, the on-average stress response profiles still hold true.

Getting your stress under control may help restore normal communication and dampen irritability, but to get to that point you'll have to commit to using some strategies of stress management.

Here are some strategies to consider and act on:

- Structured problem solving: tackling problems that give rise to stress in a thoughtful, step-by-step, constructive, and deliberate way. Writing things down on paper is best. This may also involve gaining the advice of others who can help in this process

- Daily exercise – especially before your evening meal. This can help burn off stress hormones in the bloodstream, and stimulate neurotransmitters in the brain responsible for modulating mood and emotion

- Limiting alcohol intake to a low risk level (alcohol interferes with sleep and depresses mood).

- Cutting out caffeine (caffeine acts as an unwanted stimulant and interferes with sleep; it can make stress worse)

- Slowing life down, and deliberately engaging in calming activities and recreation. Going about ordinary tasks more slowly and deliberately – *slowing physical motion* can be very effective

- Writing down what is most important to you – getting back in touch with your deepest values.

- Finding a good relaxation technique (one that works and that is easy to practice), and using it several times a day

- Learning to control your thoughts. Disciplining yourself to think rationally about challenges and problems, and avoiding:

  - Catastrophising ('this is the worst thing that could happen to me')
  - Globalising ('everything has gone wrong; nothing will help')

  Both responses generate a lot of stress. If replaced by structured problem solving, an experience and/or problem can be cut down to size. Things that are in fact going well, and options previously not recognised, can be highlighted

  Learning about stress reduction techniques. One size doesn't fit all. Discovering techniques that work for you personally

  Developing the discipline and cycle of getting to bed at night and waking in the mornings at much the same time, and making sure you get plenty of sleep

Try this simple relaxation technique (diaphragm or *'belly breathing'* as it is sometimes called*)*:

- *Breathe in slowly and fully through your nose.* Make sure your shoulders are down and relaxed. In this exercise, your stomach should expand, but your chest should rise very little. So, if you want, you can place one hand on your stomach and the other on your chest so you can feel how you are breathing.

- *Exhale slowly through your mouth.* As you breathe out, purse your lips slightly, but with your tongue and jaw relaxed. You may hear a soft 'whooshing' sound as you exhale. That's good, listen for that sound every time you practice and learn to value it as the sound of relaxation.

- *Repeat this breathing exercise for several minutes.* Make your outgoing breath as long and smooth as you can. The outgoing breath is the key to relaxation so give it your full attention and practice breathing out in a long slow controlled way and you will quickly feel the benefit.

All the above suggestions can be matched with resources readily available and downloadable from the internet. Here are some website addresses:

http://www.studygs.net/stress.htm

http://www.humanstress.ca/

http://www.webmd.com/ (search Stress)

Good Sleep is Essential to Mental Health

Having trouble getting a good night's sleep is one of the most common complaints presenting to doctors in general practice. Around 25% of Australians report suffering from a significant bout of sleep disturbance (insomnia) during their lives, with up to 12% experiencing long-term (chronic) difficulty with either getting off to sleep or staying asleep. It's certainly no fun trying to get through the day if you feel tired, emotionally flat, irritable, and unable to function well mentally.

> Around 25% of Australians report suffering from a significant bout of sleep disturbance (insomnia) during their lives.

Lack of sleep and poor quality of sleep also account for a lot of accidents, deaths and injuries. Ten percent of people with chronic insomnia experience a serious accident or injury. Fatigue and tiredness are involved in approximately 1 in 6 fatal road accidents, 52% of work-related accidents and almost 29% of accidents around the home. Staying awake for 17 hours has been shown to cause a decrease in performance comparable to a blood alcohol reading of ·05%.

The cumulative long-term effects of sleep loss and sleep difficulties have been associated with a wide range of adverse health consequences including an increased risk of hypertension, diabetes, obesity, heart attack, and stroke. Decades of research suggest that sleep loss and sleep disorders have profound and widespread effects on human health.

What appears to be little publicised, is the fact that sleep difficulties can also contribute to and worsen many mental health difficulties. Sleep deprivation can cause depression, is strongly associated with anxiety difficulties (both as a symptom of anxiety and fuelling anxiety), and can for some people who are experiencing a mental health difficulty, increase their risk of suicide.

Like other animals, humans have natural body rhythms that are regulated by a circadian clock in the brain; a clock that is linked to nature's pattern of light and darkness, and which follows a 24-hour cycle of wakefulness and sleepiness. This clock also regulates corresponding cycles in body temperature, heart rate, high and low digestive activity, and so on. That's why the human desire to sleep is greatest between midnight and six a.m.

Shift workers commonly feel drowsy at work in the night-time, and find it difficult to sleep during the day, even if they are 'dog tired,' because it is contrary to the settings of their circadian clock. In fact, such disruption causes symptoms similar to jet lag. And though one might expect the body to eventually adjust, generally it can't, and that's why so many shift workers suffer ongoing sleep problems.

Sleep is vital for allowing the body and brain time to recover from daily demands. It's during sleep that the body makes chemicals which help it grow and repair, and the immune system becomes more active to fight infection and illness. How much sleep is enough sleep? Simply, as much as is needed for you to feel and function mentally and physically well throughout the day.

What appears to be little publicised, is the fact that sleep difficulties can also contribute to and worsen many mental health difficulties. Sleep deprivation can cause depression, is strongly associated with anxiety difficulties (both as a symptom of anxiety and fuelling anxiety), and can for some people who are experiencing a mental health difficulty, increase their risk of suicide.

Sleep difficulties commonly begin during times of increased life stress or anxiety. Most people have had the experience of lying awake at night, thinking about personal, family, work or financial problems. If a stressful issue and sleeplessness persist, a person may also become preoccupied with not being able to get to sleep – setting up a vicious cycle of anxiety and increased sleeplessness, resulting in longer term or chronic sleep difficulties.

If you are sleeping poorly, these strategies might help:

- Actively manage your daytime stress
- Avoid napping during the day, and stick to regular getting up and going to bed times.
- Put the day to rest; if you've anything on your mind, write it down to be dealt with tomorrow
- Exercise regularly, but not late in the evening
- Develop a calming bedroom routine by listening to music or reading; avoid too much conversation
- Avoid caffeine after 3pm, smoking, or a heavy meal prior to bed, and keep your alcohol intake moderate – these things can interfere with sleep
- Make sure your bedroom remains dark
- If you are likely to be distracted by noise, learn to use earplugs, or try downloading a white noise application on your phone, it will help cover over sounds all night until you wake
- If you awaken too early, don't fret about it; occupy yourself with something relaxing until you feel sleepy, then try again

If you are shift worker here are some strategies that might help your sleep:

- After a night shift wear sunglasses until you get home. Bright light sends the message to your brain to be awake
- Go to sleep as soon as possible after work, and set yourself a sleep/wake routine that you stick to even on weekends
- Try to control noise and disturbances: use a "do not disturb" sign on the front door, lower the ring tone on your phone, use earplugs, try downloading a white noise application on your phone, it will help cover over sounds for the duration of your sleep, let the neighbors know your sleep routine
- Sound-insulate your bedroom, and block out all sources of light
- Avoid caffeine at least five hours before bedtime. Alcohol can disturb your sleep as well
- Have only a snack before bed, not a big meal. Have regular meal times
- Keep the room temperature cool; it will improve your sleep
- Exercise regularly after, not before sleep
- Prepare for sleep with a warm shower or bath, and use a calming music CD or relaxation technique

If, despite your best efforts, you still experience sleep problems, be sure to talk to your doctor; you may need advice on a sleep therapy.

Sleeping pills may be a temporary option, but quickly create other problems, such as dependence, and are best avoided.

Sleeping pills may be a temporary option, but quickly create other problems, such as dependence, and are best avoided.

Many factors can cause or contribute to insomnia, including medical conditions and medications; so, if these suggestions don't do the trick, talk to your doctor.

You Don't Have to Live with an Anxiety Problem

Anxiety is one of the most common and disabling mental health difficulties in the Western World. Of course, a small amount of anxiety is fine; it can sharpen the senses, and bring energy and vitality to daily tasks and activities. But for many people anxiety gets out of hand; what they experience goes beyond just being tense, extra alert, or worried. It interferes with their capacity to go about their everyday lives. In fact, for some people, anxiety is continuously distressing and debilitating – undermining their self-confidence, and affecting work, relationships, and social life.

People with significant anxiety difficulties report being unable to carry out their usual roles and tasks, to almost the same degree as people with chronic physical disorders like heart trouble, asthma, or arthritis. Most often they present to their doctor because of worrying physical symptoms – symptoms that are the result of what has been termed the *fight or flight* response, which is the body's way of dealing with impending danger. For people with anxiety difficulties, this response is

People with significant anxiety difficulties report being unable to carry out their usual roles and tasks, to almost the same degree as people with chronic physical disorders like heart trouble, asthma, or arthritis.

inappropriately triggered by situations that pose no real threat, and are generally harmless.

Difficulties of anxiety may involve episodes of unexpected panic: an excessive fear of certain objects or situations (such as social events or crowds). Anxiety may involve obsessive thoughts and compulsive or repetitive behaviour. Occurring after a highly distressing or traumatic event, it may take the form of persistent anxious arousal, irritability, a tendency to be startled easily, a re-experiencing of the trauma, and/or avoidance of things associated with the traumatic event. However, significant anxiety difficulties, commonly arise in people who are by nature worriers, with their worrying, oversensitivity and over-concern simply getting out of control.

Left unmanaged, problem anxiety will likely not only continue, but also worsen. People with moderate to severe anxiety also have a significantly increased risk of developing depression. The good news is, with therapy, the outlook for anxiety sufferers is generally very good. But, just as with depression, people with anxiety need to be actively involved in therapy, mastering new skills and adopting changes in lifestyle. With severe anxiety, medication may also sometimes be recommended to complement therapy, though this will usually be only a temporary measure.

> People with moderate to severe anxiety also have a significantly increased risk of developing depression.

Signs of a significant problem with anxiety will include one or more of the following:

- Feeling 'on edge' or 'wound up' much of the time
- Being constantly worried about a lot of things
- Feeling irritable frequently
- Being tense or nervous much of the time
- Avoiding people and social situations
- Trembling, tingling, light-headedness, dizzy spells, sweating, urinary frequency, diarrhoea
- Feeling panicky in some situations
- Sleeping poorly/having difficulty falling asleep
- Having difficulty relaxing
- Fear of appearing like a fool socially, or of drawing others attention to oneself in a social setting

- Using alcohol or sedatives to calm down or to get to sleep
- Fear of having a serious illness that the doctor can't detect
- Fear of experiencing again the feelings of a past traumatic event
- Worrying a lot about one's health
- Fear of dying, going mad, or having something bad happen
- Having thoughts that are hard to control
- Fear of being in a place that one can't get out of, or that one can't get out of without embarrassment
- Fear of germs or infection
- Compulsively checking, counting or cleaning things
- Headaches, neck aches, chest pain, joint pain, or nausea
- Tiredness or fatigue

The most favoured therapy for anxiety usually includes techniques such as:

- Learning effective relaxation and breathing control techniques, and to consciously slow down, to become anchored in and maintain calm
- Using structured problem solving to 'cut problems down to size', and put them in perspective
- Mastering anxiety through carefully graded (stepped) exposure to previously feared situations; this is well known to be successful in diminishing anxiety
- Learning ways to 'push through and past' anxiety
- Physical exercise, that can burn up stress chemicals (like adrenaline) produced by the 'fight or flight' response
- Mindfulness training: learning how to mentally focus more in the present moment and less in the past or future. This can be helpful in diminishing anxiety as well as depression.

You don't have to live with an anxiety problem. If your anxiety is severe, talk to your GP about being referred to a psychotherapist or psychologist for therapy. You can be quickly started on a path of recovery and mastery.

A list of recommended online resources to help with anxiety are included below. However, if anxiety is severe, it is best to track down a psychotherapist or psychologist who can provide professional support and therapy.

http://au.reachout.com/self-help-strategies-for-anxiety
http://www.calmclinic.com/anxiety/coping
http://www.helpguide.org/ (search Help Guide: Anxiety)

Depression: What it is and Why It Needs to be Taken Seriously

Everyone has a bad day now and then. There's no shortage of things that can leave us feeling stressed, flat as a tack, or just plain lousy. And there can be a broad range of ways in which our experience becomes difficult and renders day to day life difficult. There are situations and circumstances in which we experience heightened anxiety and changes in our mood. The problem occurs when this kind of experience persists – particularly when changes in mood, feelings and behaviours develop into depression and won't go away.

Depression is no sign of weakness, it's not a 'woman's disease', and depressed men can't just 'pull themselves together'. If you think "that would never happen to me" – think again! In most cases the onset of depression can be linked to a common event – like bereavement, relationship problems, or money troubles. But it can also happen without any apparent reason.

Though it can exist in just a mild or moderate form (which can still be very wearing and burdensome), if depression becomes severe it can be quite pervasive and disabling. Men who are deeply depressed may also be at higher risk of suicide, because depression can lead to the experience of intense desperation, a hidden pain that without treatment or therapy, may become overwhelming.

> Men who are deeply depressed may also be at higher risk of suicide, because depression can lead to the experience of intense desperation.

Depression in men is also associated with an increased risk of several other major physical health issues including: hypertension, heart disease, and stroke. It's not something to be messed with. Though men often do act to deal with their experience of depression, unfortunately they do so often by self-medicating using alcohol – which makes things considerably worse because alcohol is a depressant drug.

Depression (often confused with physical fatigue, the effects of stress, powerlessness, insomnia, or the creeping effects of drinking too much alcohol) consists of a group of symptoms that can be quite debilitating. Depression is one of the most common mental health difficulties in

Australia. And though it is common in men, twice as many women compared to men struggle with it.

While we all feel sad, moody, or low from time to time, some people experience these feelings intensely, for long periods of time and often without any apparent reason. People with depression often find it hard to function every day and may be reluctant to participate in activities they once enjoyed.

> People with depression often find it hard to function every day and may be reluctant to participate in activities they once enjoyed.

Because depression in men is less likely to be detected than in women – because the signs of depression in men are somewhat different to those in women, it is vital that plenty of time is taken by a GP, psychologist or psychotherapist to explore a man's experience before concluding that he has depression.

Many factors can contribute to depression including:

- A family history of depression
- Hormonal changes
- Emotional stress (e.g. bereavement, job loss, relationship breakdown)
- Medicines (e.g. some cancer and heart medicines)
- Medical conditions – such as thyroid and other hormone problems, or battling a chronic or terminal illness
- Personality – the type of person you are and how you respond to life events
- Social support – whether you have sufficient supportive relationships, and people around you
- Life changes – major life events such as the birth of a baby may increase the risk of developing depression

Getting the right therapy or treatment early is crucial to a person's recovery from depression. Left untreated, an episode of severe depression may last for many months. Half the people who recover from an untreated episode of depression often slip back into their former state of depression within two years of their first episode. Severe depression is a serious condition.

> Severe depression is a serious condition. However, when it is properly treated, most people can expect a full recovery.

However, when it is properly treated, most people can expect a full recovery.

Several different *antidepressant* approaches are used for tackling depression.

They include:

- Daily physical exercise – which research has found to be surprisingly effective
- Getting lots of daytime light exposure
- Psychotherapy or psychological therapy (several different approaches have been found to be helpful)
- Bright light therapy (for which an electric bright light therapy box is used)
- Sleep improvement principles and strategies
- Mindfulness and meditation practices
- Stress and anxiety management strategies
- Structured problem solving
- A daily activity schedule
- Medication for more severe forms of depression

It is also now well known that a nutritious diet, low or zero alcohol consumption, measures that can improve sleep if a person is suffering sleep disturbance or insomnia, and positive social interaction can also be significantly beneficial.

Now with some background understanding of depression, below is a basic checklist of potential signs of depression. This is no substitute for professional mapping and analysis of a person's experience, but the checklist will help you decide whether you (or on someone else's behalf) have significant grounds for concern, and have need to talk to a doctor or consult a psychotherapist or psychologist.

What depression looks like:

For more than TWO WEEKS has a person appeared to:
1. feel sad, down, or miserable most of the time?
2. lose interest or pleasure in most usual activities?

If the response to either of these questions is yes, consider the symptom checklist below. If the answer to these questions is not yes, then depression is less likely.

Has a person experienced:
3. sleep disturbance?
4. slowing down, restlessness, agitation, or needing to be excessively busy?
5. feeling tired or without much energy?
6. a loss or gain in weight, or an increase or decrease in appetite?
7. feeling worthless? OR feeling excessively guilty? OR feeling guilty about things he should not feel guilty about?
8. poor concentration, or difficulties thinking?
9. recurrent thoughts of death, or thoughts of self-harm or suicide?

Has a person appeared to:
10. have become withdrawn socially?

Has a person appeared to have been:
11. very indecisive?
12. irritable, conflictual, or angry?
13. significantly less communicative?
14. drinking more alcohol than usual?
15. impulsive, and taking more risks than usual?

As already mentioned, the experience of acute or chronic powerlessness and situational distress can often give rise to 'symptoms' that may be mistaken for depression. Hence the importance of not jumping to conclusions and taking time to examine an individual's experience and circumstances.

A severe or ongoing sense of powerlessness, can be associated with men getting to a place of feeling suicidal and thinking thoughts of suicide. Powerlessness needs to be taken seriously – just as seriously as a condition of severe depression.

Important

If you or someone you know is experiencing thoughts about self-harm or suicide, this should be taken seriously. It is important to speak to a doctor, go to a hospital accident and emergency department, or call a 24/7 emergency mental health line <u>immediately</u>. See the list at the back of this book. If you have serious concerns about your own or another person's safety, the mental health crisis line professional will also talk you through your options of what to do.

Why Self-medication is a Bad Idea for Mental Health Difficulties

Something frequently reported by women observing their male partners in distress is how they tend to elevate their consumption of alcohol, cigarettes, and coffee. These are perhaps the most common forms of self-medication used in place of more appropriate measures of self-care. The use of any of these *psycho-active* substances or recreational drugs are self-defeating when used to respond to psychological distress, stress, anxiety or depression. More often than not, when men use these substances this way, they are mostly unaware of what they are doing. What they are doing right, is *responding* to difficult experience, just with the wrong remedy, as this topic will explore revealing some surprising facts.

Alcohol

Alcohol use is a widely-accepted part of Australian culture, and it's the most commonly used mood-changing recreational drug. The misuse of alcohol is one of the chief causes of preventable death in Australia, it is significantly implicated in social and domestic violence, and has a variety of negative effects on mental health.

Alcohol is a central nervous system depressant and not a stimulant as popularly believed. It slows the activity of the central nervous system, affecting concentration and coordination, and slowing the response time to unexpected situations. It has a variety of effects which vary for each individual. In some people, it appears to give rise to aggression. In others, it has the effect of causing them to be amorous, tearful, or perhaps talkative. Even moderate inebriation tends to induce disinhibition, more intense moods and impaired judgement – which may mean that people react uncharacteristically or get involved in situations in which they wouldn't normally become involved (such as verbal and physical conflict).

While alcohol in small doses may produce relaxation, a lowering of inhibitions, feelings of confidence, and more 'outgoingness', in larger quantities it can have a significant negative impact on mental and physical health.

Alcohol is commonly used as a form of self-medication, to help with sleep, and to dampen stress and anxiety. A large number of people who suffer insomnia use alcohol as an aid to sleep. And though it is effective in inducing sleep, it impairs sleep by causing multiple awakenings during the second half of the sleep period, and causes loss of overall sleep time, and daytime drowsiness. Sleep impairment can occur even when alcohol is consumed in the afternoon. Sleep impairment can also cause depression.

Research has also now clearly revealed a cause and effect relationship between alcohol abuse and dependence, and major depression. Clearly, alcohol not only potentially makes depression worse, it can cause depression.

As for stress and anxiety, though alcohol can temporarily dampen these, both are made worse through immoderate alcohol consumption. Other negative effects include difficulties of concentration and memory, sexual dysfunction, and a variety of cancers. Worryingly, alcohol intoxication also increases suicide risk by up to 90 times in susceptible individuals.

While there is no safe level of drinking, the National Health and Medical Research Council has developed a set of guidelines to help people make choices about how much they drink and the potential risks to their health.

For healthy men and women, drinking no more than 2 standard drinks on any day reduces the lifetime risk of harm from an alcohol-related disease or injury.

Some common questions about alcohol

1. *Does drinking affect sexual performance?*

Yes. Immoderate drinking can cause sexual dysfunction. Most men are aware of the link between alcohol and erectile problems.

2. *Is beer fattening?*

Yes. Alcohol is high in calories and contains few nutrients or vitamins. Drinking beer or any other alcoholic drink adds calories to a person's diet, which can result in them gaining weight and which can lead to obesity.

3. *Can a person save up their drinks for one good session?*

No. Drinking more than 4 standard drinks on a single occasion more than doubles the relative risk of experiencing an injury in the following 6 hours. Increased health and mental health risks also ensue with this pattern of drinking.

4. *Can a person drink when on medication?*

Mixing alcohol with medications (either over-the-counter or prescription) can have unexpected and even dangerous effects. Alcohol may also affect how well the medication works. It is important to read the packaging and consumer medicines information with all medications to see if alcohol is mentioned.

5. *Can alcohol help sleep?*

No. Though alcohol may help a person to feel tired and to go to sleep, it usually causes disrupted and poor quality sleep.

6. *How does alcohol affect mental health difficulties?*

The relationship between alcohol and mental health difficulties is complex. As a general rule, they do not mix well. Alcohol can interfere with the effectiveness of many medications and can be dangerous when taken in combination with others.

7. *Is a person at risk of developing an alcohol-related problem if their family has a history of alcohol problems?*

Yes. This does not mean they will develop an alcohol-related problem, but having a family history of alcohol-related problems is one of the factors that increases the risk. The degree of risk is related to:

◆ The closeness of the relative who has the alcohol-related problem
◆ The number of relatives involved

Knowing the family's health history can be important in making informed choices about drinking and the potential risks.

8. *Can a person drink the same amount as they get older?*

The older a person gets, the less well their body can 'handle' alcohol.

Changes in the body's makeup and metabolism, and increased use of medications as a person grows older, affect the way they process alcohol. Alcohol can increase the risk of falls, accidents while driving, and suicide in older people. Some medications, when used in combination with alcohol, can also further increase these risks, as well as reduce their effectiveness or increase side-effects.

Signs of a problem with Alcohol

- Use of alcohol to cope with stress, anxiety, anger, or sleeplessness
- Regularly drinking more than 4 drinks on one occasion
- Having tried to cut down or stop drinking without success
- Sometimes failing to do what is normally expected of them because of drinking
- Feeling uneasy, guilty, or remorseful about the amount of alcohol being consumed
- Feeling especially hopeless, angry or sad, following a bout of drinking
- Behaviour after a bout of drinking that is later regretted
- Have been injured (or have injured someone else) as a result of drinking
- Drinking is followed by conflict or arguments with a partner
- Being unable to stop drinking once having started
- A friend, relative, or a doctor has expressed concerns
- Unable to remember what happened the night before because of drinking
- Sometimes start drinking early in the day as a way of 'steadying the nerves,' or getting rid of a hangover

If some of these signs are familiar it may well be time to get some professional advice. This can be done by talking to a GP and/or by going online to:

National Drugs Campaign: http://www.drugs.health.gov.au/ (Choose the Need Help tab). This site has Australia wide resources including Counselling Online details.

There are useful self-help options to be found in the book, *Taking Care of Yourself and Your Family: A Resource Book for Good Mental Health*, in the chapter titled: Alcohol. This chapter has lots of general information, and explores self-help options for alcohol reduction or cessation. There may be a copy in your local library. If not, go online to www.youcanhelp.com

Another option is to contact a State or Territory Alcohol and Drug Service.

Caffeine

Caffeine is arguably the world's most widely consumed psychoactive substance, and it is commonly consumed regularly every day in workplaces because it is an effective psychostimulant. Despite its popularity, caffeine (consumed through a range of beverages including coffee, energy drinks and tea), has a number of negative affects you might want to consider, especially if you are a person who is experiencing stress, anxiety, or insomnia. Caffeine may appear innocuous because of its popularity, but it can cause significant problems, especially used as a form of self-medication.

As the stimulant found in coffee, caffeine is commonly consumed in the morning as a pick-me-up. The way it works is to stimulate production of the hormone adrenaline. This is normally a stress-triggered hormone that is intended to heighten your physical strength and alertness for a short period of time in response to a perceived threat. This is one feature of a much broader physiological activation referred to as the 'fight or flight response'. Release of adrenaline is marked by elevated heart rate, elevated blood pressure and heightened energy. This wide-ranging systemic activation of body organs is quite unhealthy if it is a daily chronic pattern. Also, though caffeine may deliver you a quick burst of energy, it may be followed by some degree of crash, marked by fatigue and irritability.

It is worth mentioning here that some frequent consumers of caffeine, fool themselves into thinking that adrenaline fuelled energy is somehow a healthy and desirable state, one in which they are functioning at their best, including most creatively. However, functioning from a place of mindful well-slept calm is far superior to the artificial state of arousal, and without the negative health implications.

One of the problems with caffeine is that it has a long half-life, which means it stays in your blood stream a long time before being fully out of your system. Around 50% of the drug may be cleared from your body within 5-6 hours, but it may take up to a full day or more to fully eliminate it from your system.

Any caffeine in your bloodstream at bedtime may make it harder to get off to sleep, but will also disrupt the quality of your sleep by altering your sleep architecture, or the pattern of your sleep. It will reduce your rapid eye movement sleep (REM). After a disrupted sleep, you'll likely wake feeling tired. Drink coffee again to stimulate your system, and a vicious cycle begins to emerge. Sleep loss is cumulative, and even small nightly decreases can add up and disturb your daytime alertness and performance.

The direct effects of caffeine during the day, plus the added problem of caffeine related sleep deprivation can significantly add to the burden of stress and anxiety you may be experiencing, and will likely make it more difficult for you to manage strong emotions too.

Caffeine can interact with some medications and herbal supplements. For example, some antibiotics can interfere with the breakdown of caffeine (which may increase the length of time it remains in your body), and may also amplify unwanted effects of caffeine. Medication prescribed to open bronchial airways may react with caffeine causing nausea, vomiting and heart palpitations. The common supplement Echinacea, used to assist with colds and other infections, may increase the concentration of caffeine in your blood and increase the likelihood of some of caffeine's unpleasant effects, including:

◆ Insomnia
◆ Nervousness
◆ Restlessness
◆ Irritability
◆ Stomach upset
◆ Fast heartbeat
◆ Muscle tremors

Curbing your caffeine habit

It is best not to abruptly cease or too rapidly decrease your caffeine intake because you may experience withdrawal symptoms, such as headaches, fatigue, irritability and nervousness. Best to cut down slowly over a couple of weeks. Perhaps start with the rule that you don't drink any caffeine containing beverage after mid-afternoon – preferably midday.

To change your caffeine habit more gradually, consider:

- *Cutting back.* But do it gradually. For example, drink smaller and less cups of coffee each day. Or avoid drinking caffeinated beverages late in the day. This will help your body get used to the lower levels of caffeine and lessen potential withdrawal effects.

- *Keeping tabs.* Start paying attention to how much caffeine you're getting from beverages and food. Read labels carefully. Even then, your estimate may be a little low because not all foods or drinks list caffeine. Chocolate, which has a small amount, doesn't.

- *Switching to decaffeinated.* Most decaffeinated beverages look and taste the same as their caffeinated counterparts, so they are good substitute.

- *Checking the bottle.* Some over-the-counter pain relievers contain caffeine — as much as 130 mg of caffeine in one dose. Look for caffeine-free pain relievers instead.

Nicotine

Smoking is one of the leading preventable causes of death in Australia. And smoking doesn't only cause lung cancer, it causes 16 types of cancer. Tobacco smoke contains more than 7,000 chemicals, including over 70 carcinogens known to trigger cancer. Smoking is associated with impotence, heart attack, stroke, high blood pressure, emphysema, chronic bronchitis, diabetes, eye deterioration, dental and gum problems. Middle aged men who are long-term heavy smokers, have double the risk of aggressive prostate cancer. Recent research has found that smoking can alter your genes and leave a lasting effect on your DNA – making you vulnerable to cancer and other diseases.

Remember the Marlboro Man advertisements? They still feature on billboard advertising in developing countries. Well, the Marlboro man didn't get to ride off into the sunset, he died of lung cancer! Well, to be more exact, two of them did (a variety of men did the ads). Of the two that did die (that we know of), both became anti-smoking campaigners.

Doubtless you've heard all the warnings about tobacco and nicotine before. But did you know although most smokers report wanting to quit, others continue on their 'merry way' because of the belief that smoking provides them with mental health benefits. Moreover, evidence suggests that many regular smokers believe cigarettes alleviate emotional problems, feelings of depression, stress and anxiety, mood swings, and tension. Such views about smoking, of course, influence their preparedness to quit.

Well here is the irony: smokers who believe this are not only mistaken, but could likely experience improvement in their mental health by quitting the habit. Research published in the British Medical Journal showed that people who quit smoking experienced a significant drop in anxiety, depression, and stress. This effect was true for both the general population of smokers and those with a diagnosed mental health difficulty. Quitting was found to be at least as effective for alleviating depression and anxiety as taking antidepressants. Those who quit also experienced an increase in both quality of life and positive emotion. This finding swiftly demolishes any myth that smoking can contribute to improved mental health; far from it, it undermines it.

If you are a smoker, the single biggest thing you can do to improve your health is to quit. And you might just save your life as well. The benefits of quitting are almost immediate. With nicotine cleared from your system, your blood pressure will start to return to normal. Within a few days your lungs will function better, and exercise will become easier. Your sense of taste and smell will start to normalise. Within a year, your risk of lung cancer will reduce, and your risk of heart disease will be almost half that of someone who keeps smoking. You will also stop putting those around you at risk.

There's no 'right' way to quit smoking. And no matter what you do, you'll still need to be determined and to work at it. Most smokers still try to throw the habit 'cold turkey', without any help. But getting some support, and maybe medication, can improve your odds of success. Your doctor may suggest Nicotine Replacement Therapy or some other form of medication to help with physical addiction, and re-establishing abstinence after a 'slip-up'. But physical cravings are only half of the equation; psychological attachment must also be tackled. That's why, for most people, a stop smoking program which provides personal support and follow-up is best. An excellent option is the free 24/7 QUITLINE on 13 1848, offering a 12-week program.

No matter how long you have been smoking, it is well worth quitting. To plan on doing so, is a vital step in taking care of both your physical and mental health.

It's Official: Fathers Too Can Experience Postnatal Depression

Health services across Australia have been keen to improve their monitoring of mothers after childbirth, to better identify and respond to any signs of postnatal depression. This is not only for the mother's sake, but because it's now well known that postnatal depression in mothers can affect the quality of maternal care, with negative consequences for children's later social, behavioural, psychological and physical development. But recent research suggests that healthcare workers need to start seeing fathers as an important part of the equation as well, because it is estimated that around 5–7% of new fathers experience postnatal depression, and that pregnancy and childbirth are high-risk times for not only mothers but fathers too.

It is estimated that around 5–7% of new fathers experience postnatal depression, and that pregnancy and childbirth are high-risk times for not only mothers but fathers too.

Though it has been known for some time that adolescent children of depressed fathers exhibit higher rates of mental health difficulties, little was known about the potential effects of paternal depression in younger children's lives. Researchers are now saying that in fact this effect can be profound. In families where fathers experienced depression soon after the birth of their child, children assessed at age three and a half were twice as likely to have significant emotional and behavioural problems. What turned out to be most striking was that father's depression had a more significantly adverse effect on boys than girls; though the reason for this is still not clear.

Overall, these findings underline just how important it is to ensure that not only mothers but fathers too be considered and supported before and after childbirth, and that both are monitored for any early signs of depression. This needs to happen not just for the children's sake, but also for the wellbeing of both parents and their relationship.

Some common triggers for men's postnatal depression include:

- problems, fears, and anxieties surrounding the birth
- health issues of the baby
- relationship and financial difficulties
- high pressure employment
- coping difficulties after the birth
- feelings of personal inadequacy
- lack of family support

Some common symptoms of postnatal depression include:

- anxiety
- changes in mood
- irritability
- anger
- loss of motivation
- constant tiredness
- withdrawing from usual communication
- problems with sleeping
- appetite disturbance
- loss of self-confidence
- loss of interest in usually pleasurable activities;
- feelings of helplessness
- sometimes even suicidal thoughts

Overall, these findings underline just how important it is to ensure that not only mothers but fathers too be considered and supported before and after childbirth, and that both are monitored for any early signs of depression.

Treatment for depression is generally straightforward and effective. But dealing with symptoms early is always best. If you (or someone you know) have some symptoms of depression, don't wait for them to get worse. Talk to a GP, or make an appointment with a psychotherapist or psychologist for help.

Old and Grumpy Maybe, but Not Old and Depressed

For men who have reached their senior years, there are often many life events that are cause for feeling miserable and being objectionable – events that younger people are usually little aware of. Older men may have to contend with: all the adjustments of retiring from the workforce, frustrating physical limitations, temperamental or debilitating health conditions, bereavement, loss and grief, social isolation and perhaps loneliness.

Depression is not a normal part of ageing, nor is it generally more common in the elderly than for younger age groups.

Some men also must contend with the intrusiveness of home care, or leaving their own home and going into a hostel or nursing home. Any of these events can pose a huge challenge emotionally and psychologically. Yet despite what life throws at them, most elderly men cope remarkably well.

Depression is *not* a normal part of ageing, nor is it generally more common in the elderly than for younger age groups. Risk factors such as loneliness, sickness, or being in care, may trigger depression (though sometimes no trigger is apparent), but depression should never be thought of as the norm.

Symptoms suggesting the possibility of depression should always be explored and properly assessed. Depression is a mental health difficulty that can have serious consequences if it isn't recognised and treated in a timely way. It can seriously damage a person's quality of life, and adversely affect their relationships and general health. Severe depression can also be life threatening, and may lead to suicidal thoughts or even suicide. Left untreated, depression may also worsen and last longer.

Depression in older men can easily be 'masked' or hidden in amongst physical ailments and their effects.

Depression in older men can easily be 'masked' or hidden in amongst physical ailments and their effects. Some symptoms of depression like insomnia, changes in appetite, and signs of social withdrawal, though cause for concern in a younger man, are frequently disregarded in elderly men as "just old age". Depression can also be mistaken for age related changes in thinking, or even the early onset of dementia; because in common with these conditions, depression can affect memory and concentration.

Some common symptoms of depression in older men include:

- loss of self-confidence
- feeling tired all the time
- sleep disturbance
- not enjoying usual activities
- flat mood
- apathy
- not eating well or caring about personal appearance
- withdrawing from family and friends
- withdrawing from usual communication
- avoiding social events
- not getting things done that are usually important
- memory problems and confusion
- acting out of character
- irritability
- anger;
- increased use of alcohol
- unexplained physical ailments
- suicidal thoughts

If you have some symptoms of depression (or someone close to you has), don't wait for them to get worse. It's time to speak to a health professional. Experiencing suicidal thoughts should be considered serious; help should be sought immediately, by calling a doctor, going to a hospital, or phoning one of the mental health crisis line numbers (see the list in the back of this book).

Retirement and Mental Health: Waiting for God or Seizing the Day?

etirement was once little more than a chance to breathe a sigh of relief, before the final curtain. But things have changed for most men: they live longer, are more affluent and healthy, and have more choices as they enter a much lengthier period of retirement. Yet many are discovering that escaping to a life without work, albeit crammed full of activity, can resemble being stuck in an airport departure lounge waiting for a flight that never arrives.

Though choosing retirement, rather than being forced into retirement, can have far less negative consequences, both still have much in common in the unexpected ways they can impact on men. And though money may well be an issue, even men who retire with more than ample means, and who anticipate being able to do everything they never had time to do, can find themselves deeply disenchanted – even depressed. No less alarming is the frequent decline in health, and increased likelihood of hospitalisation and incapacitation following retirement, ominously referred to in common parlance as 'retirement disease'.

No less alarming is the frequent decline in health, and increased likelihood of hospitalization and incapacitation following retirement, ominously referred to in common parlance as 'retirement disease'.

For men, work isn't just a source of income, it largely defines who they are; through it men value themselves and feel valued by others. Work is generally far more central to men's sense of wellbeing than it is for women; it is a very important outlet for men's need to be productive, creative, and to remain meaningfully 'in action'. A workplace, for men, is also a vital and yet underestimated source of social interaction and social inclusion. For many men, life without work is a life with little value and meaning.

"Retirement is the ugliest word in the language," said Hemingway. He was referring to how the word and notion of retirement can be so unnecessarily life diminishing. To be suddenly exiled from the life you've invested so much in, and that has contributed so much to your self-identity, status, sense of purpose, meaning, and social belonging, is no simple change. It's a major life transition, and one that brings with it many losses to be grieved, new tasks and challenges of adjustment and adaptation, and unexpected stresses.

Realistically, the pace of life does have to change to take account of advancing years. A staggered withdrawal from the work force may well become necessary. But there's no good reason why life can't remain meaningfully intact, with a healthy momentum and continuing creative and productive engagement, so long as some measure of meaningful work remains part of the equation.

> The stage of life associated with retirement, rather than suggesting the onset of decline and disengagement, can be an opportunity to explore new possibilities and new horizons.

The stage of life associated with retirement, rather than suggesting the onset of decline and disengagement, can be an opportunity to explore new possibilities and new horizons: perhaps a new era of work – one more of choice than necessity, and a pace and type of work that is enjoyable and manageable. And far from being a retreat, it can be a sensibly refashioned and reinvigorating continuity.

Time for Soul-Searching Over Men and Suicide

You might remember Beaconsfield mine drama in Tasmania (though quite some years ago, now), which was the scene of the tragic death of one miner and the fortunate rescue of two others, prompted a media frenzy with national and international coverage. It was good, for once, to have attention drawn to the reality of what we expect so many men to do for a living – and the risks their jobs entail. However, it would be naïve to think that all the attention was because people really care about the plight of workers. TV and Media bosses, cheque books in hand, could hardly contain their impatience with the locals, who so 'inconveniently' needed to attend to their trauma and grief, before talking deals.

People were right to be so glad that two men survived against the odds, and were returned to their families. They were right to be concerned for the grieving family of the deceased miner. But while the Beaconsfield drama was being played out, another ongoing and much more consequential tragedy was unfolding: around 55 Australian men, much loved sons, brothers, husbands, fathers, uncles, and grandfathers, committed suicide. No heroic attempts to save these men. No interest in televising their stories. Perhaps these days something has to be 'newsworthy' to be deserving of attention, resources and remedy?

Currently, suicide researchers say that an average of at least 40 men die by suicide every week, over 2000 each year, representing around 75% of all suicides, and exceeding the total number of Australian road deaths.

Currently, suicide researchers say that an average of at least 40 men die by suicide every week, over 2000 each year, representing around 75 % of all suicides, and exceeding the total number of Australian road deaths. These are conservative figures since they do not account for the many suspected suicides of males that die in otherwise unexplained single vehicle single occupant car crashes.

One of the biggest obstacles to responding effectively to this issue appears to be that some academics, health professionals, and commentators, can't seem to get beyond a view of men and maleness that insists on seeing them as somehow deficient. Blaming men for "holding in their emotions" and "not seeking help", calling for changes to the traditional male role, sounds plausible but is, at best, lazy and simplistic. It's a view that avoids dealing with the more complex issues of male suicide. It's a view uninformed by the lived reality of most men's lives – what society expects of them, and what they must try to be to meet those expectations.

Blaming men for "holding in their emotions" and "not seeking help", calling for changes to the traditional male role, sounds plausible but is, at best, lazy and simplistic.

As long as men are required to police our streets, protect our borders, work on building sites, in mines and manufacturing, at sea and on land, they will need to be tough, masculine, and significantly less emotional than women – and will need to be genuinely appreciated for that.

Right now, men who are troubled need male appropriate, accessible, and non-blaming support services; the kind that know how to earn men's trust, and engage them respectfully, to be 'invited in' behind their necessary toughness, to where their personal issues and emotions await assistance.

Male suicide is commonly associated with things like: relationship breakdown, bereavement, loss of job or career, financial problems, high levels of stress and depleted emotional and personal coping resources, depression (and other mental disorders), as well as ready access to firearms, pills, or other means of committing suicide.

> Right now, men who are troubled need male appropriate, accessible, and non-blaming support services; the kind that know how to earn men's trust, and engage them respectfully.

What Men Experiencing Suicidal Thoughts Need to Hear

Suicide isn't a pleasant subject and it seems that, as quickly as it is raised and discussed publicly, a new silence closes in around it. Yet however uncomfortable we might feel about it, the tragedy of at least 40 men dying by suicide each week in Australia is simply unacceptable – as is the awful aftermath of suffering of those left to grieve and deal with often unanswerable questions for years. We need to talk about it; *we need to do something about it.*

Men who experience suicidal thoughts should be considered as being in real danger, because a significant number of those who have suicidal thoughts go on to attempt suicide, and of these the majority will die by suicide on their first attempt.

Men who are depressed need to take their condition seriously as well, because not only does depression account for suicidal thinking in many cases, men with severe depression may go on to kill themselves. Nevertheless, whilst men who are depressed are particularly at risk and need to receive timely support and assistance, many men who die by suicide have no history of depression, discernable symptoms of depression or any other mental health condition. What they often do have in common is a situational crisis, or a personal history characterised by major stressors, and the experience of powerlessness. That's why it is needful that we extricate male suicide from the exclusive *mental illness* 'frame' it has been in for too long, because in many cases, there is no basis for assuming that major depression or any other serious mental health difficulty (of a kind that is usually termed 'mental illness') is the culprit for suicide. This underlines the critical importance of mental health and other human service providers being required to understand male psychology and experience, in order to better understand and respond to the approximately 50% of their constituents that are male.

Men who experience suicidal thoughts should be considered as being in real danger, because a significant number of those who have suicidal thoughts go on to attempt suicide, and of these the majority will die by suicide on their first attempt.

This underlines the critical importance of mental health and other human service providers being required to understand male psychology and experience.

Men experiencing suicidal thoughts need to hear a number of important things:

◆ No matter how bad your situation, no matter how overwhelming your mental/emotional pain, there is always a better option than considering suicide – but it may not have occurred to you. Speak to a doctor, go to a hospital, or phone a 24/7 emergency mental health number; help and relief can quickly follow.

◆ A man who kills himself does terrible violence to his family and friends. Thinking "they'd be better off without me" doesn't cancel out the fact that they'd be greatly damaged – perhaps for life. Promise yourself (and someone else) that you'll get help, that you'll do it now, and you won't give up until you get it.

- Suicidal thinking (and the emotions tied in with it) can be driven by depression. Depression, when it is severe, can be paralysing and can 'suck the life out of you'. It certainly isn't a chosen state of mind. Risk of following through with suicide increases without treatment. Seek help immediately.

- Suicidal thinking (and the emotions tied in with it) may also be caused by feeling acutely powerless in some way, because of a situational crisis: something that has happened or is happening over which you feel you have little or no control. It may be that life feels like in too many ways it has been against you. You may not find your way out of this distress without help. Seek help immediately.

- Who are the people that really matter to you? Think about why they matter, and the good things that have happened between you.

- If you have a gun, rope, pills, or anything else you've thought of using to kill yourself, either lock them up and give the key to someone for safe keeping, or hand them over to someone, so that you're kept from harm's way until you've received help and have recovered.

- Feelings of hopelessness, helplessness, and overwhelming mental/emotional pain can be quickly turned around with appropriate help or treatment.

- Things can be made to feel and look very different; hope for the future can be restored, if you act with courage and speak to a doctor, go to a hospital, or phone a 24/7 emergency mental health number (see the list at the end of this book).

"More powerful than all problems is the courage to deal with them"

Loss and Grief: Men Often Grieve Differently to Women

How ever you choose to frame it, grief of bereavement is not the kind of experience anybody likes to have: a confusion of painful emotions, physical upheaval, having your vulnerability on public display. But grieve we must and will, because grief follows most significant losses in our lives, especially the loss of someone we've been strongly attached to. There's simply no avoiding it unless we block out our whole capacity to feel – our capacity to enjoy living and loving. Trying to keep grief at bay is just to postpone the inevitable, and invites a more overwhelming and difficult experience later; something that can have serious consequences for our mental and physical health, and relationships.

In the case of bereavement, it is quite common for men to arrive in a psychotherapy or counselling session because of concerns expressed by a female partner or family member about them not coping with the loss. Interestingly, when asked about the basis of concern, men will often say, 'she is concerned that I am not showing enough emotion', or, alternatively, though perhaps less frequently, men will say, 'she is concerned about me because I have showed a lot of emotion'. This of course represents some confusion about what male coping looks like.

> Trying to keep grief at bay is just to postpone the inevitable, and invites a more overwhelming and difficult experience later; something that can have serious consequences for our mental and physical health, and relationships.

> Every person will grieve in his or her own individual way. But it's also important to recognise that men generally grieve and mourn their losses differently to women.

Every person will grieve in his or her own individual way. But it's also important to recognise that men generally grieve and mourn their losses differently to women.

Women are usually quite adept at seeking out support for themselves and supporting each other. They tend to relieve their emotional pain through open expression of it, and by verbalising it in the company of others.

Men may have to choose more consciously to allow grief emotions to surface, and will usually need a private or 'safe' ritual space (like a cemetery, in the case of bereavement) in which to experience them, and the healing that brings. Simply *being with* a supportive male confidant (where little exchange of words occurs) or taking time out alone in the natural environment, to be open, vulnerable, and reflective, can also be very healing for men.

An effective and characteristically male way of responding to the emotions of grief is by 'pushing them out' into actions and activities – often ritualised activities. Men commonly choose to create or build something, or employ a simple ritual, to mark and value in some way (or to commemorate) the death of a person and the passing of things associated with them. Yet, however men choose to engage with their grief, express and find healing in their grief, there must always be room to 'take a break' from its intensity. Neither ignoring grief, nor remaining in it continually, best achieves healing. Taking time out to focus on the practicalities of attending to life changes, new tasks and roles, and adjustments in relationships, is also essential to healing and recovery.

Contrary to the popular view that men don't cope as well as women with bereavement and grief, research suggests that only when men are deprived of social support do they fare more poorly than women. Though men may be more naturally inclined than women to want to be alone and reflective in dealing with their grief, they still need and benefit immensely

> An effective and characteristically male way of responding to the emotions of grief is by 'pushing them out' into actions and activities – often ritualised activities.

> Research suggests that only when men are deprived of social support do they fare more poorly than women.

from the support and company of others. However, it is honest and attentive 'presence' that is often most beneficial, rather than conversation.

They may approach the task differently to women but, if men are allowed to grieve as men, by far the majority of them will manage well.

Returning to the question of what male coping looks like in bereavement and grief: men may show little emotion because their characteristic way of coping is not being verbally and emotional expressive in public. Asked how they are coping, men will generally say that when they are on their own or with a trusted male confidant, they do express emotion and do talk about their experience, although not necessarily at length.

It also needs to be remembered that that men are most often expected to be the solid *mainstay* or a *surrounding protective cordon* for their family and others in times of emotional distress. They can hardly perform this role if they themselves don't distance themselves to some degree from the emotional content of distressing situations. Should they not perform this role, those looking to them as a protective and steadying influence may become significantly more anxious and distressed.

Men are most often expected to be the solid mainstay or a surrounding protective cordon for their family and others in times of emotional distress.

More reliable signs of a man not coping adaptively with bereavement and grief might be: if he is becoming increasingly distant and withdrawn (pulling away from partner, friends, family, and activities he is usually keen on), signs of a persistent low mood, lack of energy, changes in appetite, insomnia, not acknowledging the death, perhaps becoming intentionally buried in work, or obsessively engaging in some activity to the exclusion of normal social responsibilities. If in doubt, talk to an experienced grief counsellor, psychotherapist or psychologist.

Learning How to Make Good Use of Anger

Mention anger, and people often associate it with men. Understandably, perhaps, given that it's socially more permissible for men to express anger publicly (making it more noticeable) than it is for women. But appearances can be deceptive. Behind closed doors, both men and women tend to express anger and hostility. However, this tells us little about the nature and potential of anger itself.

No human emotion is without purpose. Anger is no exception. It is a normal, natural, and very useful emotion. Granted, all too frequently it is expressed in destructive and unhelpful ways, especially in relationships – but it doesn't have to be. Its energies can be used quite beneficially.

> No human emotion is without purpose. Anger is no exception. It is a normal, natural, and very useful emotion.

We generally experience anger in situations where we feel powerless, or fear being rendered powerless in some way; or when we identify with someone else who is experiencing this. Occasions of perceived injustice, mistreatment or humiliation may produce anger. Anger can also quickly arise when we feel a lack or need of control, in a situation in which we believe it is our role to put order into disorder – such as in a crisis, where there is much emotion, an imminent danger or perceived threat.

The right use of the energies of anger is to focus them on the situation that is generating the needed resource of anger. But it's crucial not to do this until we have calmed ourselves and have a clear head. Ancient male warrior codes warn never to act in anger. They demand that the energies of anger first be harnessed, and put under the command of a calm and clear head. When we are *in* anger, we are at our weakest. When we have harnessed and taken command of its

> Ancient male warrior codes warn never to act in anger. They demand that the energies of anger first be harnessed, and put under the command of a calm and clear head.

energies, we are most potent – most able to tackle the issues that need its energies, with honesty, patience and constructiveness.

Anger can energise and motivate us to stand up for ourselves or others, and to communicate how we really feel and what we really think; it can cause us to push beyond our usual boundaries to face issues long neglected – things calling for thought, decision and action; it can take us to a place of confronting our own need to change in some important way. But its energies are wasted, if thoughtlessly hurled at others or ourselves.

Anger can energise and motivate us to stand up for ourselves or others, and to communicate how we really feel and what we really think

Here are simple rules of thumb for responding to anger:

- **STOP**, step back, calm down, and imagine harnessing anger's energies as you might harness a horse;

- **CONSIDER** the source and reason for the anger; you have to be both honest and thoughtful about this

- **ACT** to resolve or tackle the issue, but only if you are calm, and only once you have honestly considered the issue – including from the other person's (or persons') perspective. If anger re-emerges, go back to **Stop** and work through the steps again.

Surviving Separation is a Mental Health Issue

Men who go through separation often find themselves struggling with overpowering emotions, and may sometimes be prone to behavioural responses that are unhelpful to themselves and others. Men in these circumstances are at risk of a decline in their mental health and are at greater risk of suicide.

The all important thing for them to know is that they can survive if they are prepared to follow some rules of survival. This means learning to survive without over-analysing things or immediately trying to envisage a new life or relationship.

You (or someone else you know) may feel as though you're in 'free fall', and don't know what to hold on to. You may be full of pain and hurt, and just want it to stop. You feel out of control, powerless and angry, with everything seeming meaningless, and you just don't know if you can bear it.

The fact is, with basic support, it is possible to survive separation and eventually make a fresh start, even if the emotion of the moment and the grief of loss feel overwhelming. Emotions often cover over the facts, and in such circumstances, it's common to experience emotions so powerfully that reality becomes distorted, and life can't be imagined without the person/partner that has left or gone.

Here are some important rules of survival:

First rule of survival: When it comes to emotional pain, 'you can run but you can't hide'

- Better to turn and face it, acknowledging and briefly 'looking' at what is happening in your experience, but not indulging it or going over and over it unnecessarily. You'll need to learn to push past emotion and to stay committed to everyday tasks and responsibilities
- You'll need to find some healthy recreation for yourself, even if you don't feel like it

If you can't get past feeling *overwhelmed* or *desperate*, you may be potentially at risk. You'll need to talk to someone sensible and stable; you'll need to accept some support. And that doesn't mean creating a rebound relationship that you can draw on for sympathy.

Second rule of survival: Talking to a male friend could be helpful

- Men usually know how to *cut to the chase* and help other men feel back in control
- A male friend may be good at putting some masculine structure on strong feelings (where your own structure has become compromised); feelings that shouldn't be sent underground, and which need to be contained and *tamed*
- You will still need to do your own emotional homework – following rules of survival, and not expecting someone else to do this for you

Third rule of survival: Facing Facts

- Is the separation permanent? The gut wrenching stuff will not stop until this question is answered decisively
- The worst thing you can do is delude yourself about this. It's a common denial behaviour to refuse to let go of a failed relationship by hoping that a partner will change her mind – which only postpones the pain and draws out the whole process of grieving

Fourth rule of survival: Self-care

Essentials of self-care:

- Preparing properly for sleep and getting plenty of sleep. Sleep is essential for mood buoyancy, and coping
- Eating properly. Limiting sugar, eating food low in saturated fat, and eating a proper breakfast and lunch, with a lighter evening meal
- Staying close to friends and family. Coping can be greatly enhanced through positive social interaction and contact. Social withdrawal reduces coping capacity
- Getting health related exercise for 30 minutes each day
- Learning and using a relaxation technique
- Always keep yourself safe. If you feel suicidal (or are having suicidal thoughts) you need to go straight to a doctor, to a hospital, or should contact a 24/7 mental health emergency line (see the list of numbers at the back of this book). This is a not-negotiable rule of self-care

Fifth rule of survival: Making a firm decision to be disciplined

- Taking control over self-defeating thoughts. If you go over and over longing memories, feelings of regret, or thoughts of powerlessness, your ability to cope will be undermined, and you'll *drown* in the emotion these thoughts generate
- Refuse to idealise the lost relationship (if it had been perfect it wouldn't be broken and lost)
- Refuse to indulge feelings of self-pity or regret
- Stick to your decisions

Other important disciplines include:

- Avoiding alcohol. It is a powerful depressant, increases anxiety, interferes with sleep, and promotes suicidal thoughts.
- Refraining from phoning, emailing, texting or communicating with your ex-partner except when genuinely necessary.
- Being angry, but not acting in anger.

The Thorny Issue of Succession:
A Hidden Mental Health Difficulty

The proud Australian rural tradition of life on the land: of achieving an honest living, providing security for one's retirement and, through one's children, continuing a farming family tradition, is running into serious trouble these days. One of its major difficulties is the issue of succession. Few other issues so potently tap into deeply held beliefs, reservoirs of emotion, and generational differences in aspirations and expectations. Few other issues seem so able to plunge families into self-devouring and destructive animosity.

No longer can it be taken for granted that mum and dad will stay on the farm until retirement, with children taking over the running of the property and supporting them during retirement, until eventually inheriting the property on their demise.

For one thing, people of the younger generation are much less prepared to stay on the farm, or invest themselves and their efforts, without a clear succession plan. The mere possibility, or waiting and trusting that succession will occur, competes poorly with the broader range of options that young people (who are often well educated) now have available to them. Given the increasing complexity of farming, and the accompanying stress of operating in financially pressured and uncertain times, the new generation of farmers may also have much less compunction than their predecessors in opting out of farming to pursue other opportunities. An associated issue is the difficulty of single males finding suitable partners in rural communities, due to a diminishing population of available females.

With fewer children remaining on or having an attachment to farm properties, there is a heightened likelihood of claims being made upon the assets of the family farm by siblings, who may wish to claim what they consider to be their rightful portion of the assets. The increased likelihood and implications of relationship breakdown and divorce must also be reckoned with; occurring not only in the relationships of children and their respective partners (with a common fear being that a daughter-in-law might "run off" with half the farm), but in those of parents as well. In view of all these potential issues, the importance of proper succession planning cannot be overstated.

Succession planning involves frank family discussion, and negotiations requiring sophisticated communication skills. It also requires diligent consideration of various legislation, such as the Administration and Probate Act, the Inheritance (Family Provision) Act, the De facto Relationships Act, Family Law Act, and provisions of welfare and taxation legislation – any of which may affect the rights of people who have an interest in the farm and its assets. Consequently, effective succession planning will almost always involve drawing together financial planning, mediation, and legal expertise and support.

Perhaps that all sounds a bit daunting? Well, a simple first step may be to consult a Rural Financial Counsellor. They can assist with the coordination of the whole process – including recommending and/ or arranging for the involvement of other skilled financial and legal practitioners.

Emergency Mental Health Numbers

There are significant differences between the mental health crisis support and information services offered by Australian States and Territories. The following telephone numbers may serve as a 'first port of call' for emergencies and enquiries:

SA   Ph: 13 1465 Rural and Remote Mental Health Service

VIC   Ph: 13 6169

TAS   Ph: 03 6233 2388

WA   Ph: 1300 555 788

NT   Darwin Ph: 08 8999 4988

    Alice Springs Ph: 08 8951 7535

ACT   Ph: 02 6205 1065 or 1800 629 354

QLD   Ph: Accident and Emergency Department at nearest hospital

NSW   Locate the Mental Health Crisis number in the front of your area telephone directory, or ring Lifeline on 13 11 14.

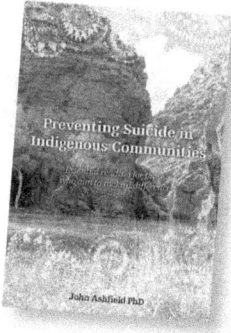

Preventing Suicide in Indigenous Communities

Essential reading for those who aim to make a difference

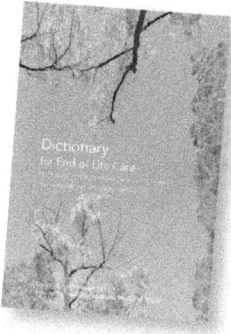

Dictionary
for End of Life Care

The language of medicine and medications made simple

For non-medical staff, carers and volunteers

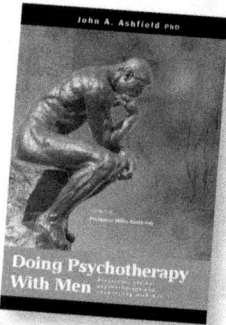

Doing Psychotherapy With Men
Practicing ethical psychotherapy and counselling with men

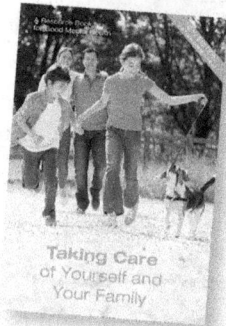

Taking Care
of Yourself and Your Family

Available at:

Website: www.youcanhelp.com.au **Email:** info@youcanhelp.com.au

www.ingramcontent.com/pod-product-compliance
Lightning Source LLC
Chambersburg PA
CBHW050602280326
41933CB00011B/1947